GRAPHIC STANDARDS OF SOLAR ENERGY

SPRUILLE BRADEN III

LIBRARY OF CONGRESS CATALOGING IN PUBLICATION DATA

BRADEN, SPRUILLE, 1953–
    GRAPHIC STANDARDS OF SOLAR ENERGY.
    INCLUDES INDEX.
    1. SOLAR HEATING--GRAPHIC METHODS.
    2. SOLAR HOUSES--DESIGN AND CONSTRUCTION--
       GRAPHIC METHODS.
    I. TITLE
    TH7413.B7   697'.78   77-122117
    ISBN 0-8436-0166-3

CBI PUBLISHING COMPANY INC.
221 COLUMBUS AVENUE
BOSTON, MASSACHUSETTS 02116

TABLE OF CONTENTS

TO MY PARENTS
ELDA AND SPRUILLE

FOREWORD

ENERGY DEMAND HAS EXCEEDED ITS SUPPLY IN THE UNITED STATES SINCE THE MID 1960'S. DURING THIS TIME THE NORTH-EASTERN SECTOR OF THE COUNTRY WAS STRUCK WITH THE "GREAT BLACKOUTS". HOWEVER, THIS TYPE OF ENERGY SHORTAGE IS NOT LIMITED TO THAT AREA. IN 1973 2 MILLION PERSONS RESIDING ALONG FLORIDA'S GOLD COAST WERE AFFECTED BY PROLONGED ELECTRICAL BLACKOUTS. A DIFFERENT KIND OF SHORTAGE TOOK PLACE IN 1973 AND 1974 WHEN THE MAJORITY OF OUR POPULATION AND A LARGE SECTION OF OUR ECONOMY SUFFERED THE EFFECTS OF THE OIL EMBARGO. ANOTHER EXAMPLE OF UNMET ENERGY DEMAND TOOK PLACE IN 1977 WHEN OVER 3 MILLION

PERSONS WERE UNEMPLOYED AS A DIRECT RESULT OF THE LIMITED AVAILABILITY OF NATURAL GAS.

THE UNITED STATES BUREAU OF MINES ESTIMATED THE KNOWN GLOBAL RESERVES OF NATURAL GAS AND PETROLEUM TO LAST 38 AND 31 YEARS RESPECTIVELY, IF THEIR RATE OF CONSUMPTION WERE TO REMAIN AT THE 1970 LEVELS. THE RAPIDLY DIMINISHING RESERVES AND THE INCREASED DEMAND FOR ENERGY ARE EXPECTED TO DRIVE FOSSIL FUEL PRICES UP TO AN ALL TIME HIGH. UNAVOIDABLY, HOWEVER, THERE WILL COME A POINT IN TIME WHEN REGARDLESS OF THE PRICE CONSUMERS ARE WILLING TO PAY, THERE WILL SIMPLY BE NO FOSSIL FUELS TO BE SOLD.

WITHIN THIRTY YEARS THE UNAVAILABILITY OF CONVEN-
TIONAL ENERGY SOURCES, SUCH AS OIL AND NATURAL GAS,
WILL FORCE THE PRODUCTION OF CHEAP ALTERNATIVE
ENERGIES. THIS WILL BE FURTHER ENCOURAGED BY THE
NEED TO AVOID SOCIAL AND ECONOMIC CRISES BROUGHT
ABOUT BY SEVERE DECLINES IN AGRICULTURAL AND INDUS-
TRIAL PRODUCTIVITY.

THE USE OF ALTERNATIVE NON-POLLUTING ENERGIES AND
THE OVERALL CONCEPT OF ENERGY CONSERVATION ARE NO
LONGER ISSUES OF THE FUTURE. THEY HAVE BEEN WITH US
FOR YEARS AND WILL BECOME AN EVER MORE IMPORTANT PART
OF OUR LIVES, REGARDLESS OF THE STANDARD OF LIVING

WE CHOOSE TO MAINTAIN.

AN OVERWHELMING CONTRIBUTION TO THE UNITED STATES'
SOCIAL AND ECONOMIC WELL-BEING CAN BE MADE IN THE
FIELDS OF ENERGY CONSCIOUS DESIGN AND SOLAR ENERGY.
ENERGY CONSCIOUS DESIGN FREES FUEL SUPPLIES WHICH
CAN BE USED TO POWER CERTAIN ASPECTS OF OUR INDUSTRY
VITAL TO OUR ECONOMY. SOLAR ENERGY IS CLEAN, FREE
AND INEXHAUSTABLE. IT OFFERS THE OPPORTUNITY TO BREAK
FREE FROM THE DEPENDENCE ON FOREIGN ENERGY SOURCES.
THE PURPOSE OF THIS BOOK IS TO ASSIST IN THE DESIGN
AND MAINTENANCE OF SOLAR POWERED AND ENERGY SAVING
BUILDINGS.

ACKNOWLEDGEMENTS

FIRST AND FOREMOST I WISH TO THANK MR. FORREST WILSON. IT IS BECAUSE OF HIS KEEN FORESIGHT, RECEPTIVENESS AND CONSTANT ENCOURAGEMENT, THAT THIS BOOK HAS COME TO BE.

EXTENSIVE THANKS ARE DUE TO MR. RICHARD WEIL AND MS. DESIRÉE HOLIBOWICZ. THEIR GENEROUS HELP AND ADVICE GREATLY FACILITATED THE WRITING, EDITING AND PRODUCTION OF THE MANUSCRIPT.

I ALSO WISH TO THANK MR. RAY SLUZAS FOR HIS ADVICE, MR. MICHAEL APARICIO FOR HIS SUPPORTIVE RESEARCH, MR. RAYMOND SULLIVAN FOR HIS EFFORTS IN THE PRODUCTION OF THE DESIGN CHECK LIST, MR. TIMOTHY CROSBY FOR HIS HELP, AND MS. LYNN TAYLOR FOR HER PATIENCE AND HELP IN COORDINATING AND EDITING THE FINAL COPY.

INTRODUCTION

SPECIFIC DESIGN INFORMATION FOR THE DESIGN AND MAINTENANCE OF SOLAR ENERGIZED AND ENERGY SAVING BUILDINGS IS PRESENTED IN THIS BOOK.

THE INFORMATION IS PRESENTED GRAPHICALLY. THERE-FORE IT IS MOST IMPORTANT TO PURSUE THE UNDERSTAND-ING OF EACH SKETCH, SINCE THEY ARE THE MAIN TEXT. THE USER, WITH REASONABLE UNDERSTANDING OF THE CONCEPTS PRESENTED, SHOULD BE ABLE TO MAKE DESIGN DECISIONS WHICH WILL PRODUCE ENVIRONMENTALLY RESPONSIVE BUILDINGS.

THE ORDER IN WHICH THE INFORMATION IS PRESENTED SUGGESTS A SPECIFIC SEQUENCE FOR ANALYSIS AND DESIGN. THIS SEQUENCE IS RECOMMENDED FOR USERS WHO DO NOT HAVE PREVIOUS EXPERIENCE IN ARCHITECTUR-AL SOLAR DESIGN.

FOR THOSE NEEDING SEVERAL RULES OF THUMB, A DESIGN CHECKLIST BASED ON CLIMATIC REGIONS IS PROVIDED.

PART I CLIMATIC FACTORS

THIS PART INTRODUCES THE USER TO THE CLIMATIC FACTORS WHICH INFLUENCE ARCHITECTURAL DESIGN. IT HAS BEEN DIVIDED INTO THREE MAJOR SECTIONS: SUN, WIND AND WATER. THE USER IS PRESENTED WITH THE PRINCIPLES AND MECHANICS ON WHICH THE FACTORS OPERATE, HOW THE PHENOMENA ARE MEASURED AND RECORDED, HOW TO READ AND USE THIS INFORMATION.

SUBSEQUENT PARTS AND SECTIONS ARE STUDIED IN VIEW OF HOW THESE CLIMATIC FACTORS AFFECT THE PERFORMANCE OF THE VARIOUS ARCHITECTURAL AND MECHANICAL ELEMENTS.

OBTAINING A THOROUGH UNDERSTANDING OF THE CONCEPTS GOVERNING THE CLIMATIC FACTORS WILL FACILITATE AND EXPEDITE THE DESIGN SEQUENCE.

SECTION 1   THE SUN

SINCE THE BEGINNING OF TIME THE SUN HAS INDIRECTLY PROVIDED ALMOST ALL OF MAN'S ENERGY REQUIREMENTS. THE CHEMICAL REACTIONS WHICH FORMED COAL, PETRO- LEUM, AND GAS (FOSSIL FUELS) WERE STIMULATED MILLIONS OF YEARS AGO BY THE SUN.   THE SUN'S HEAT CONSTANTLY EVAPORATES THE EARTH'S WATERS WHICH RETURN TO THE EARTH AS RAIN TO FEED THE STREAMS AND RIVERS.   THESE IN TURN ARE USED TO POWER THE HYDROELECTRIC PLANTS.   THE SUN INTERACTS WITH THE EARTH'S ATMOSPHERE TO PRODUCE WINDS.   THEY PROVIDE POWER THROUGH WINDMILLS.

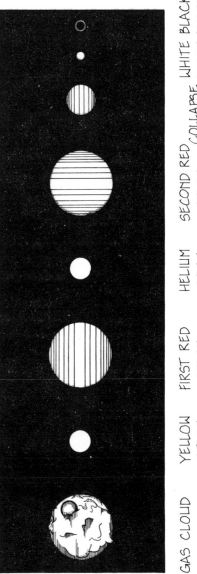

FIG. 1.1 EVOLUTION OF A SUN-SIZE STAR

GAS CLOUD   YELLOW   FIRST RED   HELIUM   SECOND RED   WHITE BLACK
STAGE   STAGE   STAGE   STAGE   DWARF DWARF

SOLAR ANGLES

THE LOCATION OF THE SUN WITHIN THE SKY VAULT CAN BE PREDICTED BY CALCULATION, BY MODEL STUDY, OR THROUGH THE USE OF SUN PATH DIAGRAMS. THESE DIAGRAMS ARE THE MOST PRACTICAL GRAPHIC METHOD FOR ACCURATELY LOCATING THE SUN'S POSITION AT ANY DATE AND HOUR.

THE SUN'S LOCATION IS MEASURED IN DEGREES. THE BEARING ANGLE "A" MEASURES THE DISPLACEMENT FROM THE SOUTH MERIDIAN. THE ALTITUDE ANGLE "B" MEASURES THE DISPLACEMENT FROM THE GROUND PLANE AT THE OBSERVING LOCATION.

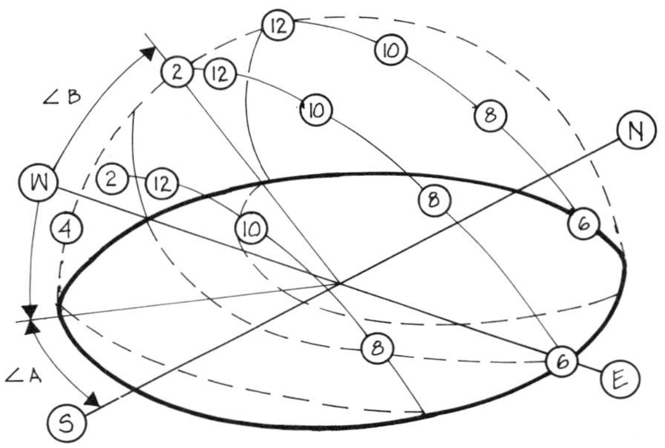

FIG.1.2 HALF-SPHERE PLOT OF THE SKY VAULT AND SUN PATHS.

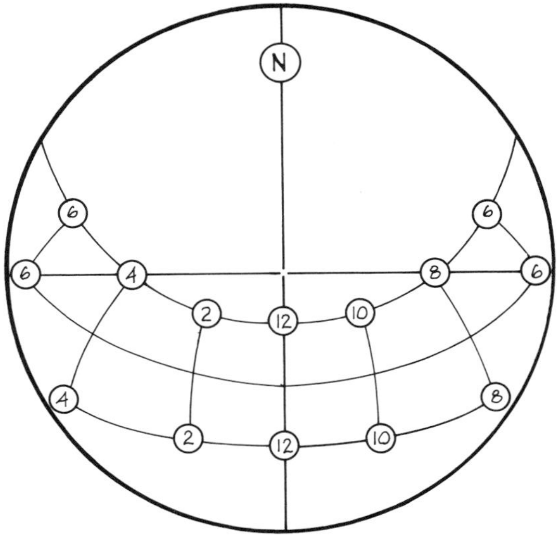

FIG.1.3 SUN PATH DIAGRAM.

SUN PATH DIAGRAM

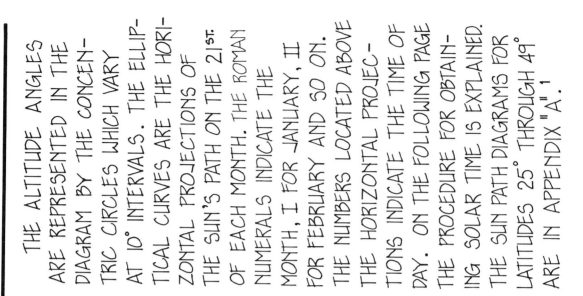

THE ALTITUDE ANGLES ARE REPRESENTED IN THE DIAGRAM BY THE CONCENTRIC CIRCLES WHICH VARY AT 10° INTERVALS. THE ELLIPTICAL CURVES ARE THE HORIZONTAL PROJECTIONS OF THE SUN'S PATH ON THE 21ST. OF EACH MONTH. THE ROMAN NUMERALS INDICATE THE MONTH, I FOR JANUARY, II FOR FEBRUARY AND SO ON. THE NUMBERS LOCATED ABOVE THE HORIZONTAL PROJECTIONS INDICATE THE TIME OF DAY. ON THE FOLLOWING PAGE THE PROCEDURE FOR OBTAINING SOLAR TIME IS EXPLAINED. THE SUN PATH DIAGRAMS FOR LATITUDES 25° THROUGH 49° ARE IN APPENDIX "A".[1]

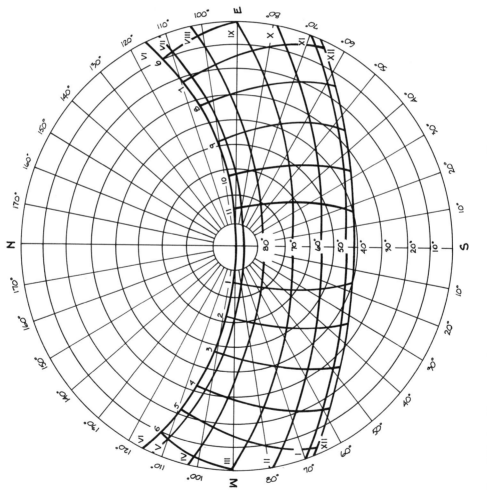

FIG. 1.4 SUN PATH DIAGRAM, LATITUDE 24°N.

FOR CONVERTING TIME INTO
SOLAR TIME:

1. IF DAYLIGHT SAVINGS TIME
IS IN EFFECT SUBTRACT ONE
HOUR FROM LOCAL TIME.

2. SUBTRACT 4 MINUTES FOR
EVERY DEGREE OF LONGI-
TUDE IF SITE IS WEST OF
CENTRAL LONGITUDE, OR
ADD 4 MINS. FOR EVERY
DEGREE OF LONGITUDE IF
SITE IS EAST OF IT.

3. CORRECT TIME VARIATIONS
FOR DAY AND MONTH, ADD
OR SUBTRACT MINS. AS
INDICATED IN THE CHART.

LATITUDE: CURVED HORIZON-
TAL LINES.

LONGITUDE: STRAIGHT VER-
TICAL LINES.[2]

JAN. 21 −11.4	APR. 21 +1.2	JULY 21 −6.2	OCT. 21 −15.3
FEB. 21 −13.8	MAY 21 +3.6	AUG. 21 −3.1	NOV. 21 −14.1
MAR. 21 −7.4	JUNE 21 −1.5	SEPT. 21 +6.8	DEC. 21 +2.0

PACIFIC STANDARD   MOUNTAIN STANDARD   CENTRAL STANDARD   EASTERN STANDARD

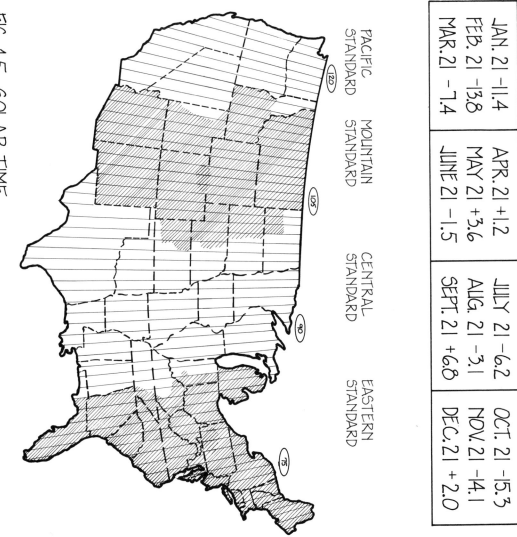

FIG. 1.5   SOLAR TIME

SHADING MASK PROTRACTOR

SHADING MASK PROTRACTORS ARE USED TO PREDICT THE EFFECTS OF SHADING DEVICES. THE EFFECTS CAN BE PLOTTED IN THE SAME WAY THE SUN PATH DIAGRAM WAS PLOTTED. THE MASK IS A GEOMETRIC PROJECTION; THEREFORE, IT CAN BE USED FOR ANY LATITUDE. BY TRACING THE MASK AND LAYING IT OVER THE PROPER SUN PATH DIAGRAM, THE USER CAN PREDICT THE SHADOWS.³

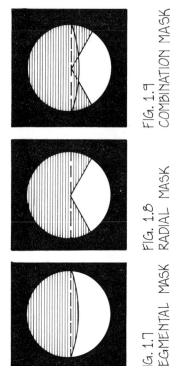

FIG. 1.7
SEGMENTAL MASK

FIG. 1.8
RADIAL MASK

FIG. 1.9
COMBINATION MASK

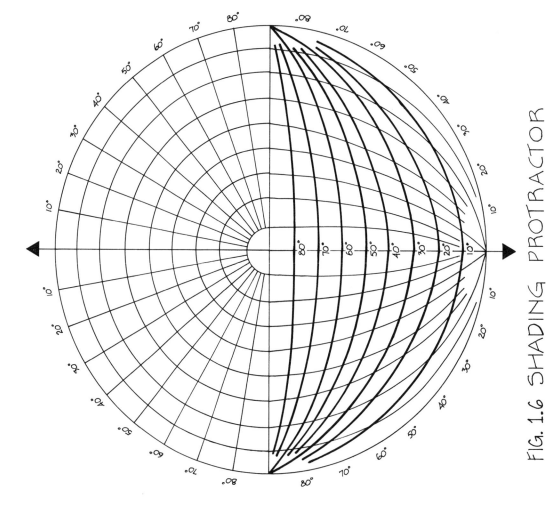

FIG. 1.6 SHADING PROTRACTOR

ISOGONIC CHART

THE SOLID LINES REPRE-
SENT THE COMPASS DEVIATION
FROM TRUE NORTH. IF THE LINE
IS LABELED "E", IT INDICATES
THE COMPASS DEVIATES TO
THE EAST. IF THE LINE IS
LABELED "W", IT DEVIATES TO
THE WEST. THE NUMBER
ACCOMPANYING THE LETTER
INDICATES THE DEGREES OF
DEVIATION FROM TRUE NORTH. FIG. 1.10 ISOGONIC CHART

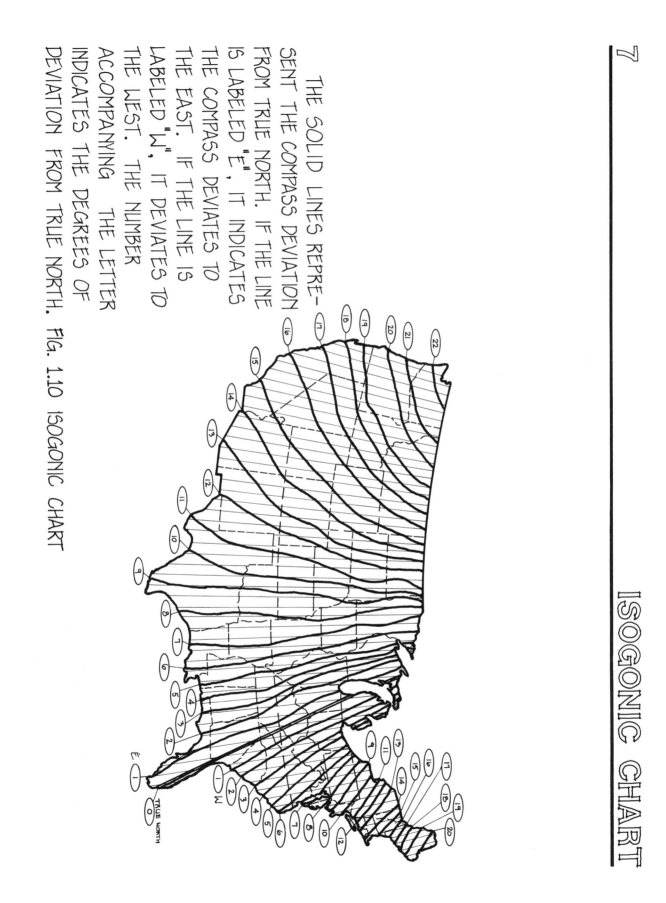

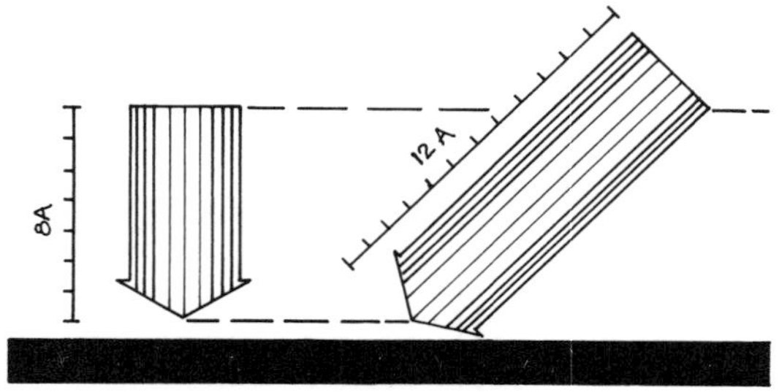

SUNSHINE CONSISTS OF ELECTROMAGNETIC WAVES TRAVELING THROUGH SPACE AT 186,000 MILES PER SECOND. IT ARRIVES AT THE EDGE OF OUR ATMOSPERE CARRYING 428 BTU'S PER HOUR FOR EVERY SQUARE FOOT OF AREA. THIS IS KNOWN AS THE SOLAR CONSTANT.

IT IS IMPORTANT TO NOTE THE DIFFERENCE BETWEEN SOLAR RADIATION AND LIGHT. LIGHT IS RADIATION IN THE REGION BETWEEN ULTRA VIOLET AND INFRARED. RADIATION IS ABSORBED INTO THE ATMOSPHERE AS A PRODUCT OF CLOUD COVER, DUST, AIR IMPURITY AND GEOGRAPHICAL LOCATION. THE LONGER THE RADIATION HAS TO TRAVEL IN THE AIR, THE MORE IT WILL BE ABSORBED INTO THE ATMOSPHERE. THIS IS WHY HIGH ALTITUDES RECEIVE MORE RADIATION AS SHOWN IN FIG.1.11

THE AVERAGE AMOUNT OF RADIATION REACHING THE EARTH'S SURFACE IS 58.5 BTU'S PER SQUARE FOOT PER HOUR, CONSIDERABLY LESS THAN THE SOLAR CONSTANT. INSOLATION SHOULD BE MEASURED AS DIRECT AND DIFFUSED RADIATION. HOWEVER, THE GREAT MAJORITY OF THE INSOLATION DATA HAS BEEN RECORDED AS TOTAL

FIG.1.11 LENGTH OF TRAVEL

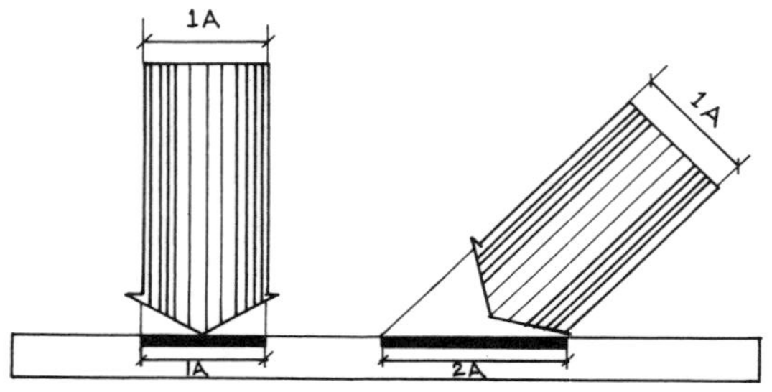

FIG.1.12 INSOLATION ON A HORIZONTAL SURFACE

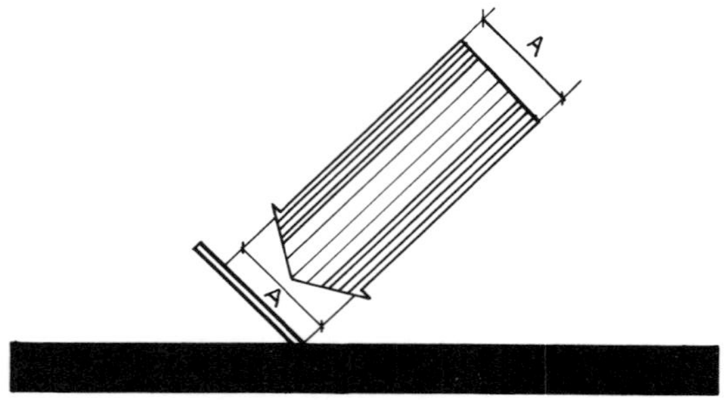

FIG.1.13 INSOLATION ON A SLOPED SURFACE

RADIATION RECEIVED ON A HOR-
IZONTAL SURFACE. FIG. 1.12
AND FIG. 1.13 SHOW HOW THE
AMOUNT OF DIRECT RADIATION
RECEIVED IS INCREASED BY
FACING THE SURFACE SOUTH-
WARD AND TILTING IT TO THE
APPROPRIATE ANGLE.

IN FIG. 1.14 WE SEE THE
RELATIONSHIP BETWEEN HEAT-
ING DEMAND AND SOLAR SUP-
PLY. IT USES HOURS OF SUN-
SHINE AS UNITS OF INSOLA-
TION. THE LARGER THE
NUMBER, THE LARGER THE
HEATING SYSTEM REQUIRED.

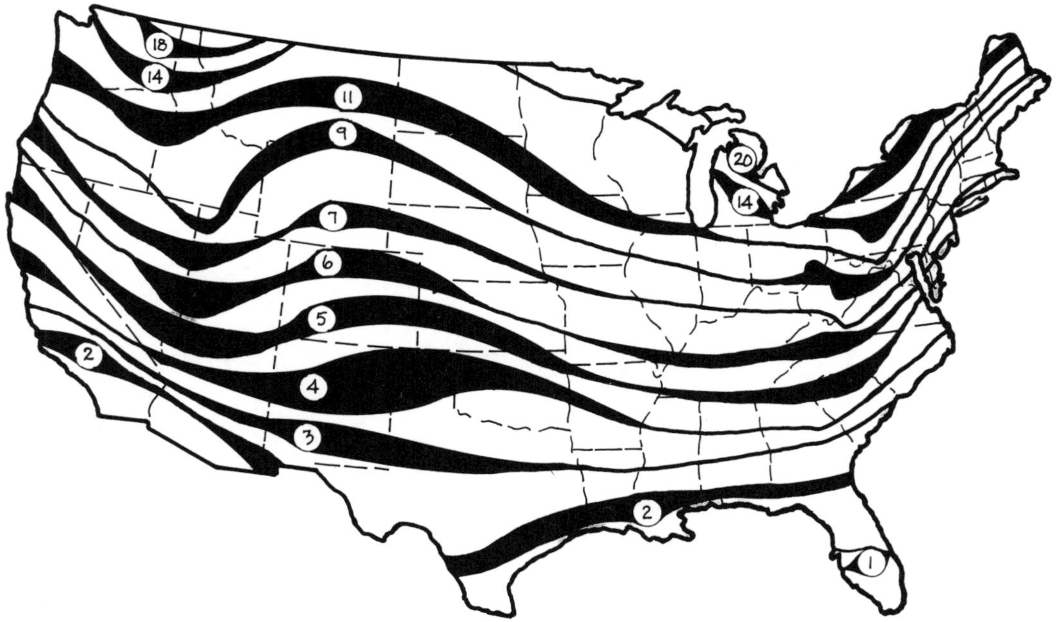

FIG. 1.14 DEGREE DAYS PER SUNSHINE HOUR

MEAN DAILY SOLAR
RADIATION PER MONTH INDI-
CATES THE AVERAGE DAILY
TOTALS OF DIRECT AND DIF-
FUSED RADIATION RECEIVED
IN A GIVEN LOCATION ON A
HORIZONTAL SURFACE DUR-
ING THE MONTH.

THIS TYPE OF MAP
SHOULD ONLY BE USED TO
GAIN A GENERAL IDEA OF
THE AVAILABLE AMOUNTS
OF SOLAR RADIATION.

A COMPLETE SET OF
MAPS ILLUSTRATING THE
MEAN DAILY SOLAR RADIA-
TION PER MONTH IS PRE-
SENTED IN APPENDIX "B".

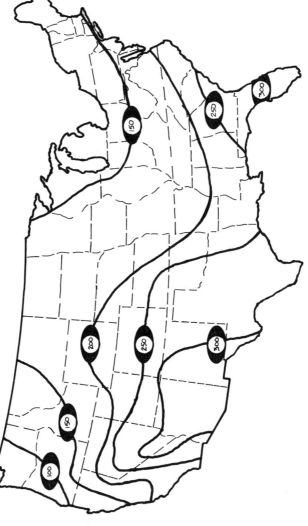

FIG. 1.15 MEAN DAILY SOLAR RADIATION IN
LANGLEYS FOR JANUARY

HEATING AND COOLING DEGREE DAYS

DEGREE DAYS IS AN EXPRES-SION RELATED TO HEATING AND COOLING LOADS. IT IS DEFINED AS THE NUMBER OF FARENHEIT DE-GREES ABOVE OR BELOW A PRE-DETERMINED LEVEL. HEATING DEGREE DAYS ARE MEASURED AS THE TOTAL NUMBER OF DEGREES BELOW 65° F. ON A GIVEN DAY. BY ADDING HOURLY TOTALS WE OBTAIN DEGREE DAYS PER MONTH. THE ADDITION OF DAILY TOTALS YIELDS HEATING DEGREE DAYS PER YEAR.[5] THIS INFORMATION IS USED WHEN CALCULATING THE ANNUAL HEATING OR COOLING LOADS OF A BUILDING.

WHEN THE TEMPERA-TURE IS ABOVE 65° F. THE HOURLY COMPONENT IS COMPUTED AS ZERO. FIG. 1.16 NORMAL TOTAL HEATING DEGREE DAYS BASE 65° F. FOR JAN.

CLIMATIC REGIONS

A CLIMATIC REGION IS A GEOGRAPHICAL AREA WITH CERTAIN PREDOMINANT CLIMATIC CHARACTERISTICS. HOWEVER, THESE CHARACTERISTICS ARE NOT UNIFORM WITHIN, OR BETWEEN, REGIONS. THE REGIONS ARE NOT DIVIDED BY A PRECISE LINE, BUT RATHER, THEY GENERALLY MERGE OVER A BORDER AREA. FOR OUR PURPOSE AND DEGREE OF ACCURACY IT IS SUFFICIENT TO DIVIDE THE UNITED STATES INTO FOUR MAIN CLIMATIC AREAS.

THE COOL REGION HAS A TEMPERATURE WHICH RANGES FROM 10°F. IN THE WINTER TO 90°F. IN THE SUMMER. THE WINTERS ARE VERY COLD AND THE SUMMERS TEMPERATE. THIS REGION RECEIVES LESS RADIATION THAN ANY OTHER PLACE IN THE COUNTRY. ITS WINDS ARE PER-SISTENT AND GENERALLY OUT OF THE NORTHWEST OR SOUTHEAST.

THE TEMPERATE REGION IS ①COOL ②TEMPERATE ③HOT-HUMID ④HOT-ARID
CHARACTERIZED BY HOT
SUMMERS AND COLD WINTERS.
CONSIDERABLE PRECIPITATION
AND HIGH HUMIDITY CAUSE
PROLONGED PERIODS OF
CLOUDY, OVERCAST DAYS.

THE HOT AND ARID REGION
ENJOYS LONG PERIODS OF
CLEAR SKIES WITH A PRE-
DOMINANTLY DRY ATMOS-
PHERE. ITS WINDS ARE
ALONG THE EAST-WEST AXIS.

THE HOT AND HUMID REGION
HAS HIGH TEMPERATURES AND
CONSISTANT HIGH HUMIDITY.
WIND VELOCITIES AND DIREC-
TIONS VARY DRASTICALLY.
HURRICANES AND TROPICAL
STORMS ARE COMMON. 6

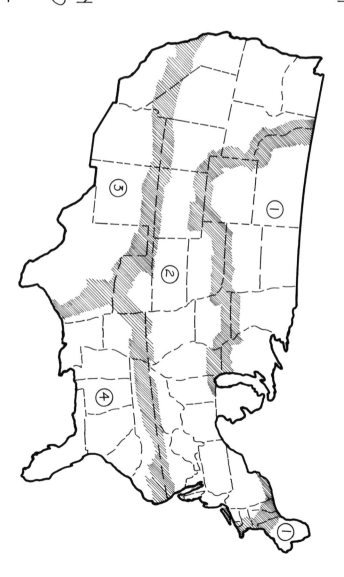

FIG. 1.17 CLIMATIC REGIONS IN THE UNITED STATES

BEAUFORT NUMBER	M.P.H.	EFFECTS
0	0	CALM, SMOKE RISES VERTICALLY
1	1-3	LIGHT AIR.; SMOKE DRIFT INDICATES DIRECTION, SEA VERY FLAT
2	4-7	LIGHT BREEZE.; WIND FELT ON FACE.; VANES BEGIN TO MOVE. SMALL WAVELETS, NOT BREAKING.
3	8-12	GENTLE BREEZE.; LEAVES, SMALL TWIGS IN CONSTANT MOTION; CRESTS OF SMALL WAVELETS BEGIN TO BREAK.
4	13-18	MODERATE BREEZE.; DUST, LEAVES AND LOOSE PAPER RAISED UP. NUMEROUS WHITECAPS.
5	19-24	FRESH BREEZE.; SMALL TREES IN LEAF BEGIN TO SWAY; FORCE OF WIND FELT ON BODY. MODERATE WAVES, SPRAY.
6	25-31	STRONG BREEZE.; LARGER BRANCHES OF TREES IN MOTION; DIFFICULT TO WALK STEADY. WHITECAPS EVERYWHERE.
7	32-38	NEAR GALE.; WHOLE TREES IN MOTION, RESISTANCE FELT WHEN WALKING AGAINST WIND. SEA HEAPS UP, WHITE FOAM FROM BREAKING WAVES BEGINS TO BE BLOWN.
8	39-46	GALE.; TWIGS AND SMALL BRANCHES BROKEN OFF TREES, WALKING PROGRESS IMPEDED. MODERATELY HIGH WAVES OF GREATER LENGTH, EDGE OF CREST BREAKS INTO SPINDRIFT.
9	47-54	STRONG GALE.; SLIGHT STRUCTURAL DAMAGE OCCURS, SLATE BLOWN FROM ROOFS, PEOPLE BLOWN OVER BY GUSTS. HIGH WAVES, SPRAY REDUCES VISIBILITY.
10	55-63	STORM; SELDOM OCCURS OVER LAND, TREES BROKEN OR UPROOTED. CONSIDERABLE STRUCTURAL DAMAGE.

WIND IS THE MOVEMENT OF AIR ACROSS THE EARTH'S SURFACE. IT IS A PRODUCT OF THE SUN'S ENERGY HEATING AIR AND EARTH. THE REGION DISTRIBUTION OF THIS ENERGY FROM WARM TO COOLER AREAS CREATES WINDS. A COMMON WAY TO CLASSIFY WINDS IS BY THEIR SPEEDS, AS SHOWN IN FIG. 2.1.[7]

FIG. 2.1 WIND FORCE

WIND DIRECTION

WIND DIRECTION GENERALLY FOLLOWS SEASONAL PATTERNS. ALTHOUGH MAPS ILLUSTRATING WIND PATHS ARE AVAILABLE, THE USER SHOULD OBTAIN INFORMATION WHICH APPLIES SPECIFICALLY TO THE SITE SINCE TOPOGRAPHIC CHARACTERISTICS OFTEN CHANGE THE PREVAILING WIND PATTERNS.

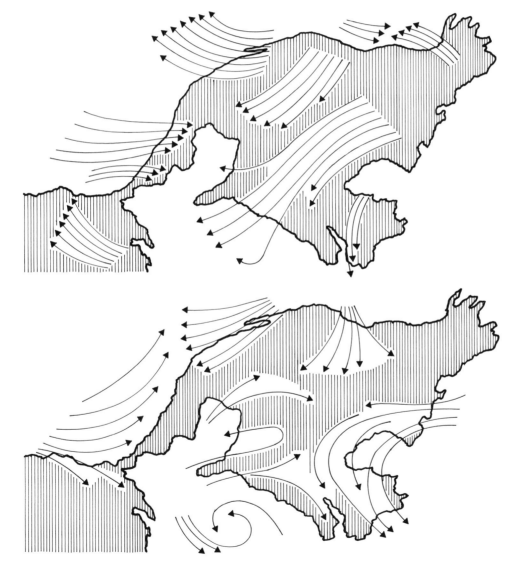

FIG. 2.2 SURFACE WINDS IN JANUARY

FIG. 2.3 SURFACE WINDS IN JULY

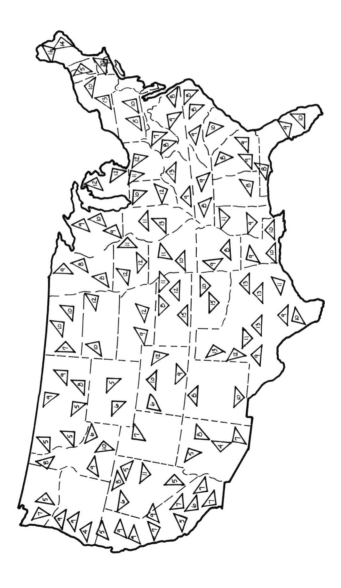

FIG. 2.4 PREVAILING WIND DIRECTION AND MEAN SPEED IN JANUARY 8

UNITED STATES SUMMER WINDS

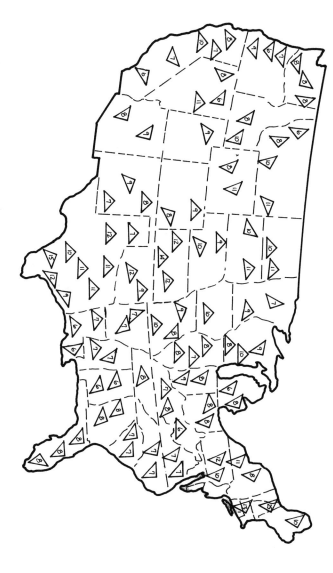

FIG. 2.5 PREVAILING WIND DIRECTION AND MEAN SPEED IN JULY

WIND SPEED AND DIRECTION
ARE RECORDED AT THREE HOUR
INTERVALS. TEN YEAR AVER-
AGES ARE PLOTTED AS WIND
ROSES. A WIND ROSE SHOWS
THE PERCENTAGE OF TIME THE
WIND BLOWS FROM THE SIXTEEN
COMPASS POINTS. IT MAY
ALSO SHOW THE PERCENTAGE
OF TIME THE WINDS ARE
CALM. WINDS WITH SPEEDS
OF UP TO THREE MILES PER
HOUR ARE CONSIDERED TO BE
CALM.

IN FIG. # 2.6 THE WIND ROSE
SHOWS THE WIND COMING FROM
THE NORTH 15 PERCENT OF THE
TIME AND BEING CALM 5 PER-
CENT OF THE TIME.[10]

① PERCENT OF TIME ② PERCENT OF TIME ③ PERCENT OF TIME ④ PERCENT OF TIME
WITH CALMS UP   WITH WINDS 4 TO   WITH WINDS 16 TO   WITH WINDS
TO 3 M.P.H.   15 M.P.H. FROM   31 M.P.H. FROM   OVER 32 M.P.H.
                     EACH DIRECTION   EACH DIRECTION   1 %
                     INDICATED.   INDICATED.   2 %

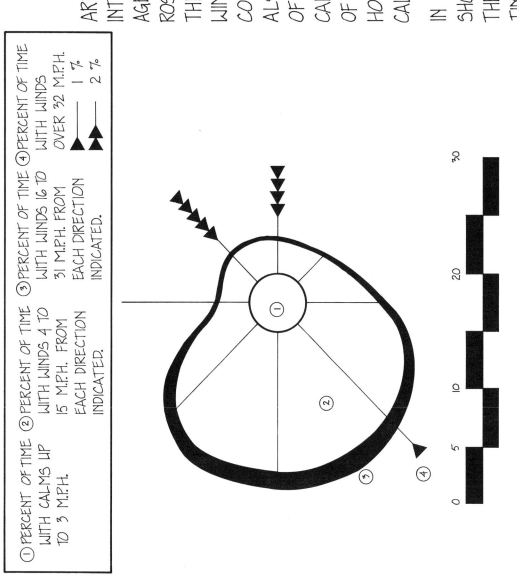

FIG. 2.6 WIND ROSE

WIND SPEED AND FREQUENCY

ANNUAL PERCENTAGE FREQUENCY OF WIND BY SPEED GROUPS AND THE MEAN SPEED

	0-3 MPH	4-7 MPH	8-12 MPH	13-18 MPH	19-24 MPH		0-3 MPH	4-7 MPH	8-12 MPH	13-18 MPH	19-24 MPH		0-3 MPH	4-7 MPH	8-12 MPH	13-18 MPH	19-24 MPH
ALA. BIRMINGHAM	27	22	30	17	3	KY. LEXINGTON	8	25	39	22	6	OHIO COLUMBUS	26	23	29	18	4
ALASKA ANCHORAGE	28	35	25	11	2	LA. NEW ORLEANS	16	27	32	19	5	OKLA. OKLAHOMA CITY	2	11	34	34	13
ARIZONA PHOENIX	38	36	20	5	1	MAINE PORTLAND	10	30	33	22	4	OREG. PORTLAND	28	27	25	16	4
ARK. LITTLE ROCK	12	30	39	16	2	MD. BALTIMORE	7	24	39	22	6	PA. PITTSBURGH	12	26	34	22	4
CALIF. BAKERSFIELD	35	30	24	10	1	MASS. BOSTON	3	12	33	35	12	R.I. PROVIDENCE	11	20	32	28	7
COLO. COLORADO SPRINGS	9	27	38	19	6	MICH. DETROIT	8	23	37	26	5	S.C. CHARLESTON	12	28	35	19	4
CONN. HARTFORD	13	26	32	24	6	MINN. MINNEAPOLIS	8	21	34	28	9	S. DAK. RAPID CITY	15	22	28	21	10
D.C. WASHINGTON	11	26	35	22	5	MISS. JACKSON	33	25	26	14	2	TENN. NASHVILLE	21	31	25	14	2
DEL. WILMINGTON	15	31	30	19	4	MO. KANSAS CITY	9	29	35	23	5	TEXAS AUSTIN	13	25	34	23	5
FLA. JACKSONVILLE	10	33	35	18	3	MONT. GREAT FALLS	7	19	24	24	15	UTAH SALT LAKE CITY	12	33	36	14	4
GA. ATLANTA	13	24	36	21	6	NEBR. OMAHA	12	17	29	24	11	VERMONT BURLINGTON	24	24	28	22	2
HAWAII HONOLULU	9	17	27	32	12	NEV. LAS VEGAS	18	26	25	20	8	VA. RICHMOND	14	37	36	11	1
IDAHO BOISE	15	30	32	18	4	N.J. NEW JERSEY	11	25	34	24	5	WASHINGTON SPOKANE	17	38	27	14	3
ILL. CHICAGO	8	22	33	27	8	N. MEX. ALBUQUERQUE	17	36	26	13	5	W. VA. CHARLESTON	29	37	25	8	1
IND. EVANSVILLE	19	23	32	21	5	N.Y. ALBANY	23	24	27	21	4	WIS. GREEN BAY	8	22	32	26	10
IOWA DES MOINES	3	17	38	29	10	N.C. CHARLOTTE	20	32	31	14	2	WYO. CASPER	8	16	27	27	13
KANS. TOPEKA	11	19	30	27	10	N. DAK. BISMARK	14	20	27	24	12	PACIFIC WAKE ISLAND	1	6	27	48	17

Fig. 2.7 11

PRECIPITATION IS DEFINED AS WATER THAT FALLS ON
THE EARTH'S SURFACE IN THE FORMS OF RAIN,
SNOW OR SLEET. PRECIPITATION IS OUR MAIN WATER SUPPLY.
IN ONE YEAR THE UNITED STATES RECEIVES ENOUGH WATER
TO COVER THE ENTIRE COUNTRY WITH A 30 INCH DEEP
LAYER, OR 4,300 BILLION GALLONS PER DAY.

TOPOGRAPHY PLAYS A MAJOR ROLE IN SECURING THE
WATER ABUNDANCE FOR A REGION. ALL PRECIPITATION
IN THE U.S. ENDS EITHER IN THE ATLANTIC OR PACIFIC
OCEANS. THE ROCKY MOUNTAINS CONSTITUTE THE BOUND-
ARY BETWEEN THE TWO DRAINING SYSTEMS.

AVERAGE ANNUAL PRECIPITATION

THE AMOUNT OF PRECIPI-
TATION ON A SPECIFIC AREA
VARIES. HOWEVER, YEARLY
AVERAGES WITHIN A SPECIFIC
REGION ARE MORE OR LESS
CONSTANT. THIS AVERAGE
DIFFERS FROM REGION TO
REGION. THE DIFFERENCE IS
DUE TO TOPOGRAPHICAL VARI-
ATIONS AND THEIR EFFECTS
ON MOISTURE AND AIR FLOW.

IT IS IMPORTANT TO STUDY
THE REGIONAL PRECIPITATION
PATTERNS SINCE THEY WILL
GREATLY AFFECT THE CLIMA-
TIC CONDITIONS AND THE
HUMAN COMFORT ZONE. [12]

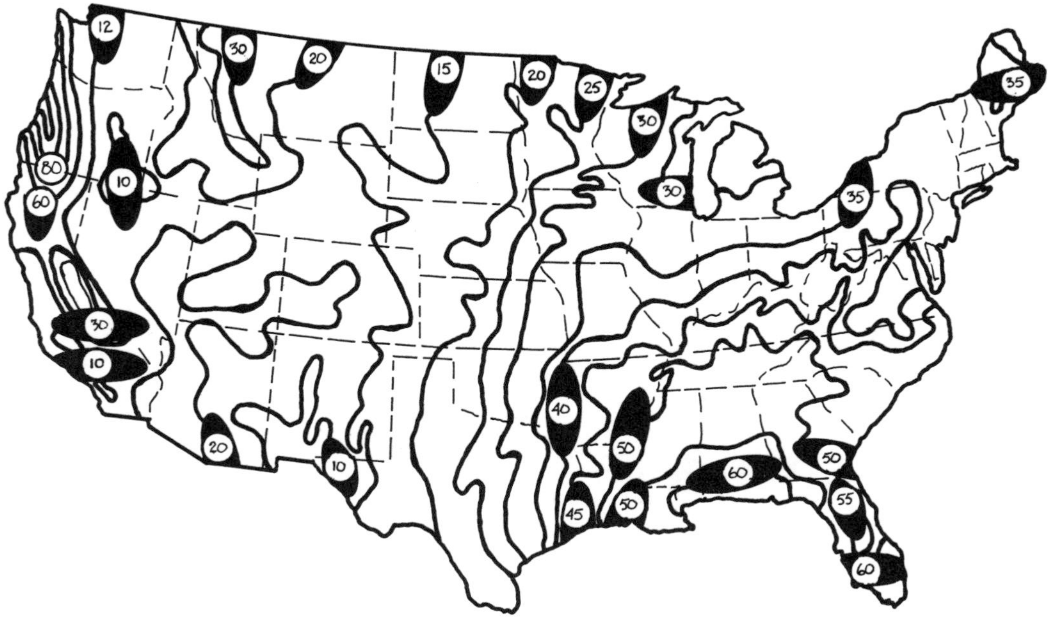

FIG. 3.1   AVERAGE ANNUAL PRECIPITATION IN INCHES

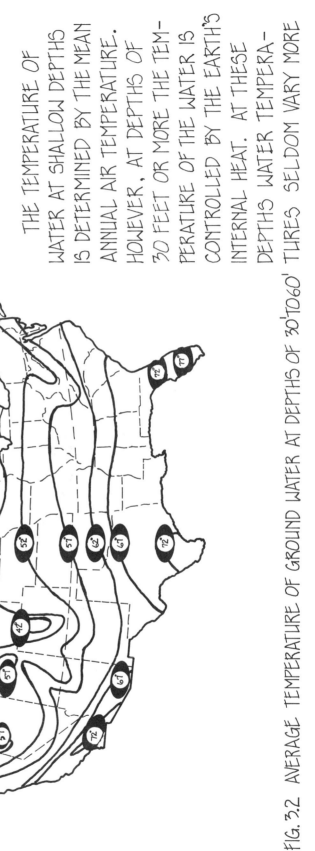

THE TEMPERATURE OF
WATER AT SHALLOW DEPTHS
IS DETERMINED BY THE MEAN
ANNUAL AIR TEMPERATURE.
HOWEVER, AT DEPTHS OF
30 FEET OR MORE THE TEM-
PERATURE OF THE WATER IS
CONTROLLED BY THE EARTH'S
INTERNAL HEAT. AT THESE
DEPTHS WATER TEMPERA-
TURES SELDOM VARY MORE

FIG. 3.2 AVERAGE TEMPERATURE OF GROUND WATER AT DEPTHS OF 30' TO 60'

THAN ONE OR TWO DEGREES
DURING THE YEAR.[13] THIS
CHARACTERISTIC IS PARTIC-
ULARLY USEFUL WHERE
WATER IS USED FOR HEAT-
ING OR COOLING PURPOSES.
THE POTENTIAL USE OF
THIS TEMPERATURE DIFFER-
ENCE CAN BE STUDIED IN
FIG. 3.2 AND FIG. 3.3.[14]

FIG. 3.3

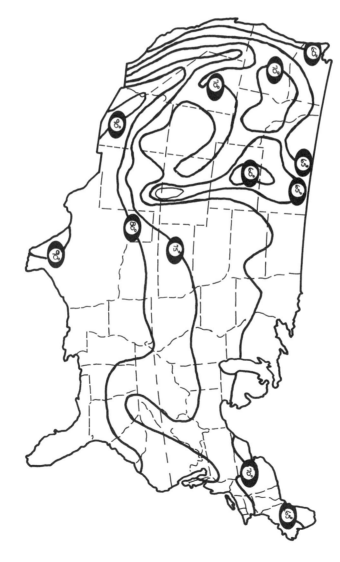

FIG. 3.3 TEMPERATURE OF SURFACE WATER IN JULY AND AUGUST

BY DEFINITION, SPRINGS ARE BODIES OF WATER THAT EMANATE NATURALLY AT THE EARTH'S SURFACE. THEY ARE GENERALLY FOUND ON HILLSIDES AND NEAR LAKES WHERE THE TOPOGRAPHY INTERSECTS THE WATER TABLE. REGULAR SPRINGS YIELD WATER AT AVERAGE GROUND TEMPERATURES. THERMAL SPRINGS YIELD WATER AT ABNORMALLY HIGH TEMPERATURES.

THE COMBINED OUTPUT OF ALL THERMAL SPRINGS IN THE UNITED STATES HAS BEEN ESTIMATED AT 500,000 GALLONS PER MINUTE. MONTANA HAS THE LARGEST THERMAL SPRING IN THE NATION, "WARM SPRING". IT PROVIDES 80,000 GALLONS PER MINUTE AT A TEMPERATURE OF 68°F.

THERE ARE OVER 200 THERMAL SPRINGS IN THE UNITED STATES. THE MAJORITY OF WHICH ARE NOT USED FOR THEIR

ENERGY CAPABILITIES BUT RATHER FOR HEALTH PURPOSES. THE UNITED STATES HAS NOT MADE ANY RECOGNIZABLE EFFORT TO TAP THESE SPRINGS AS AN ALTERNATE ENERGY SOURCE.

ON THE OTHER HAND, THE GOVERNMENTS OF GREENLAND AND NEW ZEALAND USE THEIR SRINGS TO SUPPLY A MAJOR PERCENTAGE OF THEIR ENERGY.

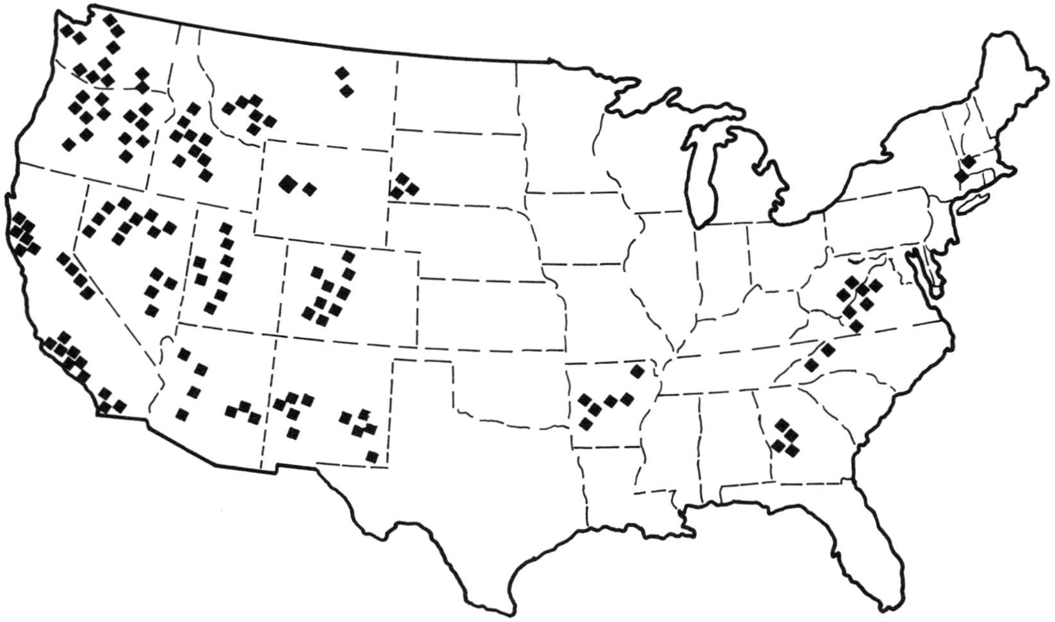

FIG. 3.4   THERMAL SPRINGS

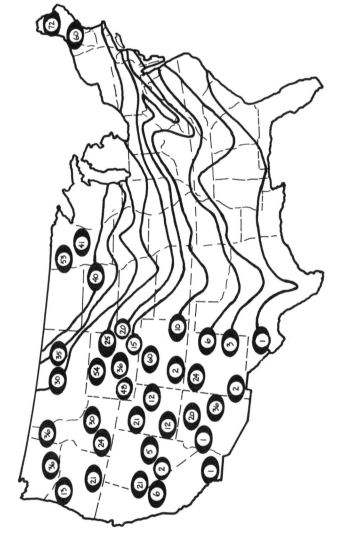

FROST PENETRATION IS CONTROLLED IN THE MOUNTAINOUS REGIONS BY ALTITUDE AND IN THE LOW CENTRAL AND EASTERN STATES BY LATITUDE.

WHEN FROST PENETRATION EXTENDS OVER LONG PERIODS OF TIME, WATER FROM OTHER FORMS OF PRECIPITATION TENDS TO RUN OFF THE FROZEN SURFACE. THIS PREVENTS WATER SEEPAGE INTO THE GROUND WHICH RESTRICTS THE REPLENISHMENT OF STORED GROUND WATER.[16]

FIG. 3.5 AVERAGE DEPTH OF FROST PENETRATION

SNOWFALL INCREASES IN NORTHERN LATITUDES AND WITH HIGHER ALTITUDES. IT IS A PRODUCT OF LOW ATMOSPHERIC TEMPERATURES.

THE SOUTHERN CALIFORNIA COASTAL ZONE AND THE GULF OF MEXICO RARELY EXPERIENCE SNOWFALLS. ON THE OTHER HAND, NORTHERN NEW ENGLAND AND THE GREAT LAKES AREA ARE ACCUSTOMED TO HEAVY LEVELS OF SNOWFALLS. THE WESTERN UNITED STATES HAS HIGHLY IRREGULAR SNOWFALL PATTERNS.

SNOW IS IMPORTANT IN THE ARID REGIONS BECAUSE IT SUPPLIES MOISTURE BANKS WHEN IT MELTS IN THE SPRING.[17]

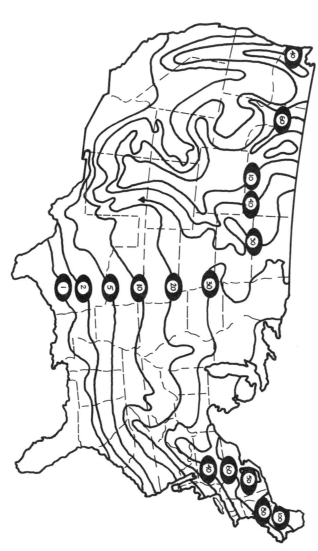

FIG. 3.6 AVERAGE ANNUAL SNOWFALL IN INCHES

PART II ENERGY CONSCIOUS DESIGN

THIS PART OF THE BOOK INTRODUCES THE READER TO ENERGY CONSCIOUS DESIGN THROUGH THE MANIPULATION OF ARCHITECTURAL ELEMENTS. EMPHASIS IS PLACED ON THE PROPER USE OF INSULATION SINCE IT IS THROUGH THIS PRACTICE THAT ENERGY WASTE CAN BE REDUCED BY AS MUCH AS 40%.

THIS PART HAS BEEN DIVIDED INTO FOUR MAJOR SECTIONS: SITE DEVELOPMENT AND BUILDING INTEGRATION, BUILDING'S INTERIORS, BUILDING'S COMPONENTS, AND DESIGN CHECKLIST. EACH SECTION IS STUDIED IN VIEW OF HOW CLIMATIC FACTORS AFFECT THEIR OPERATION. THE DESIGN CHECKLIST PROVIDES GENERAL RULES AND DESIGN GUIDELINES FOR EACH CLIMATIC REGION.

SECTION 4 SITE DEVELOPMENT

EACH SITE HAS ITS OWN UNIQUE CLIMATIC AND TOPOGRAPH-
IC CHARACTERISTICS. IT IS AROUND THESE CONDITIONS
THAT THE DESIGN PROCESS MUST EVOLVE. A SYMPATHETIC
RESPONSE TO THE PARTICULAR SITE LIMITATIONS WHICH UTIL-
IZE THE NATURAL RESOURCES AND INTEGRATE THEM INTO
THE DESIGN WILL BRING ABOUT AN ENERGY EFFICIENT STRUC-
TURE.

THE MAIN GOAL OF THE ENERGY CONSCIOUS DESIGNER IS
TO CONDITION THE INTERIOR ENVIRONMENT TO SUPPORT A
LEVEL OF CLIMATIC COMFORT ACCEPTABLE TO THE USERS
WHILE MINIMIZING ALL TYPES OF WASTE.

ALTHOUGH EACH BUILDING SHOULD BE DESIGNED FOR ITS
SPECIFIC SITE, IT IS POSSIBLE TO FORMULATE GENERAL
RULES AND METHODS FOR SITE DEVELOPMENT AND BUILDING
INTEGRATION. IN THE FOLLOWING SECTION THESE RULES AND
METHODS ARE EXPLORED IN A CONCEPTUAL BASIS. THE DE-
SIGNER SHOULD BE ABLE TO USE THESE PRINCIPLES TO DE-
RIVE SPECIFIC APPLICATIONS.

TOPOGRAPHY INFLUENCES ALL ASPECTS OF OUR CLIMATE. MOUNTAINS AFFECT CLIMATE TO A GREATER EXTENT THAN ANY OTHER TOPOGRAPHIC ELEMENT. THEIR INFLUENCE UPON PRECIPITATION AND TEMPERATURES IS HEAVILY MARKED. ON THE AVERAGE, MOUNTAINOUS REGIONS RECEIVE TWICE AS MUCH SNOW AS THE LOW LANDS.

FIGURES 4.1, 4.2, 4.3 AND 4.4 ILLUSTRATE HEAT TRAPS, OR SUN POCKETS, WHICH WHEN LOCATED ON THE SOUTHERN SIDE OF THE SITE, OR BUILDING, CAN BE USED TO RETAIN HEAT, ESPECIALLY DURING THE COLDER MONTHS.

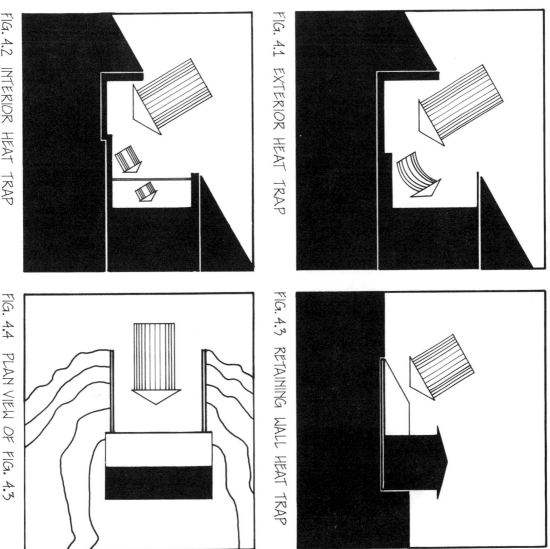

FIG. 4.1 EXTERIOR HEAT TRAP

FIG. 4.2 INTERIOR HEAT TRAP

FIG. 4.3 RETAINING WALL HEAT TRAP

FIG. 4.4 PLAN VIEW OF FIG. 4.3

SOIL TYPES

IT IS NECESSARY TO SURVEY THE SOIL TO DETERMINE ITS STRENGTH, BEARING CAPACITY AND TYPE. THESE CHARACTERISTICS VARY EVEN WITHIN THE SAME SITE. AS SOIL TYPES VARY, SO DO THEIR THERMAL CHARACTERISTICS. THESE SHOULD BE STUDIED WHEN SPECIFYING INSULATION FOR FOUNDATIONS, SLABS ON A GRADE AND BASEMENT WALLS.

FIG. 4.5 THROUGH FIG. 4.8 ILLUSTRATE THE REFLECTIVE CHARACTERISTICS OF DIFFERENT SOILS.

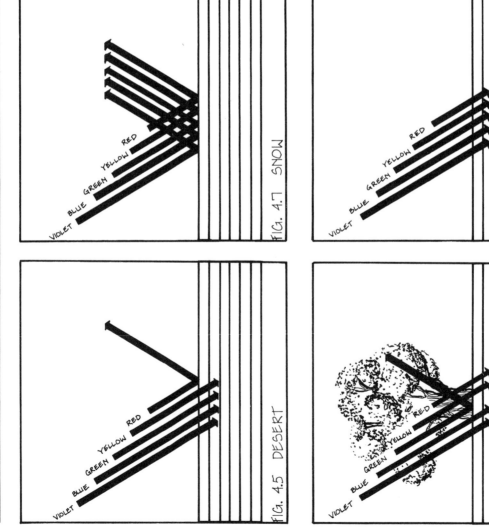

FIG. 4.5 DESERT

FIG. 4.6 FOREST

FIG. 4.7 SNOW

FIG. 4.8 PLOWED FIELD

LIGHT OBSTRUCTION

WITH THE ALTITUDE AND
BEARING ANGLES OBTAINED
FROM THE SUN PATH DIAGRAMS,
THE SHADOW PATTERNS OF
THE BUILDING'S SURROUND-
ING OBJECTS CAN BE PLOT-
TED. (SEE APPENDIX "A").

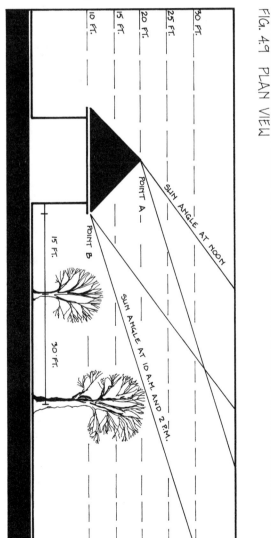

FIG. 4.10 ELEVATION VIEW

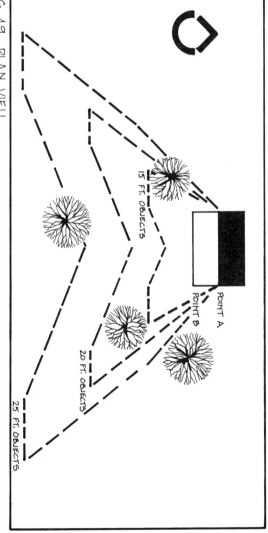

FIG. 4.9 PLAN VIEW

DECIDUOUS TREES PROVIDE FULL SHADE IN THE SUMMER AND PARTIAL SHADE IN THE WINTER. ON THE OTHER HAND, CONIFEROUS TREES PROVIDE SHADE ALL YEAR ROUND. SEE FIG. 4.10 AND FIG. 4.11.

IF THE TREE IS LOCATED AT AN APPROPRIATE DISTANCE FROM THE BUILDING, IT WILL NOT PROVIDE IT WITH A SUMMER SHADE NOR WILL IT INTERRUPT THE WINTER SUN. SEE FIG. 4.12.

FIG. 4.10 DECIDUOUS TREE - WINTER

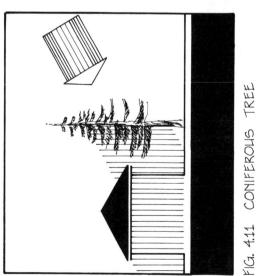

FIG. 4.11 CONIFEROUS TREE

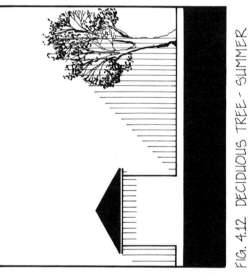

FIG. 4.12 DECIDUOUS TREE - SUMMER

TYPES OF VEGETATION

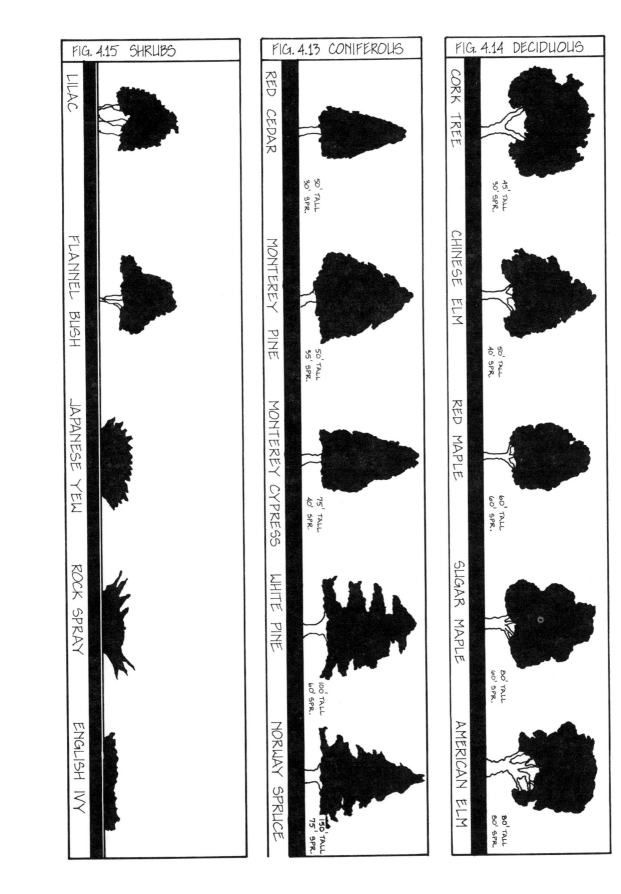

FIG. 4.14 DECIDUOUS

CORK TREE — 45' TALL 30' SPR.

CHINESE ELM — 50' TALL 40' SPR.

RED MAPLE — 60' TALL 60' SPR.

SUGAR MAPLE — 80' TALL 60' SPR.

AMERICAN ELM — 80' TALL 80' SPR.

FIG. 4.13 CONIFEROUS

RED CEDAR — 50' TALL 30' SPR.

MONTEREY PINE — 50' TALL 35' SPR.

MONTEREY CYPRESS — 75' TALL 40' SPR.

WHITE PINE — 100' TALL 60' SPR.

NORWAY SPRUCE — 150' TALL 75' SPR.

FIG. 4.15 SHRUBS

LILAC

FLANNEL BUSH

JAPANESE YEW

ROCK SPRAY

ENGLISH IVY

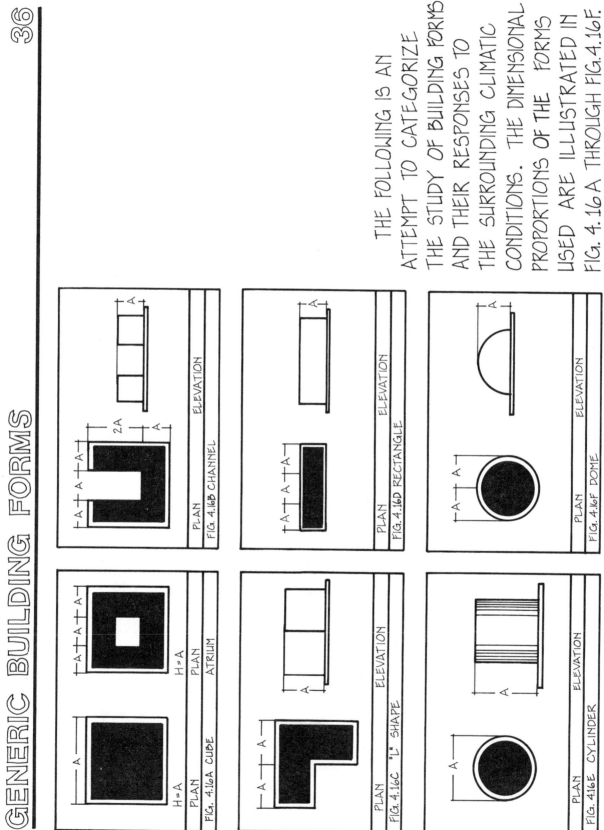

THE FOLLOWING IS AN
ATTEMPT TO CATEGORIZE
THE STUDY OF BUILDING FORMS
AND THEIR RESPONSES TO
THE SURROUNDING CLIMATIC
CONDITIONS. THE DIMENSIONAL
PROPORTIONS OF THE FORMS
USED ARE ILLUSTRATED IN
FIG. 4.16 A THROUGH FIG.4.16F.

PLAN ELEVATION
FIG. 4.16B CHANNEL

PLAN ELEVATION
FIG. 4.16D RECTANGLE

PLAN ELEVATION
FIG. 4.16F DOME

PLAN
FIG. 4.16A CUBE

PLAN ELEVATION
FIG. 4.16C "L" SHAPE

PLAN ELEVATION
FIG. 4.16E CYLINDER

FIG. 4.17 PRESENTS A COMPARISON BETWEEN THE FLOOR AREA, EXTERIOR SURFACE AREA AND THE INTERIOR VOLUME OF THE VARIOUS GENERIC FORMS. IT IS IMPORTANT TO OBSERVE THE DRASTIC REDUCTION THAT TAKES PLACE IN THE EXTERIOR SURFACE AREA AND THE INTERIOR VOLUME WHEN THE SQUARE FOOTAGE IS DIVIDED INTO TWO LEVELS. EXTERIOR AREA CALCULATIONS DO NOT INCLUDE SURFACE AREAS RESTING ON THE GRADE.

TOTAL FLR. AREA		1000 SQ. FT.				1500 SQ. FT.				2000 SQ. FT.			
NUMBER OF FLOORS	*	1		2		1		2		1		2	
		EXTERIOR SURFACE	INTERIOR VOLUME	SURFACE	VOLUME	SURFACE	VOLUME	SURFACE	VOLUME	SURFACE	VOLUME	SURFACE	VOLUME
CUBE		5,000	31,623	2,500	11,180	7,500	58,094	3,750	20,540	10,000	89,443	5,000	31,623
ATRIUM		3,000	11,180	2,500	7,906	4,500	20,540	3,750	14,524	6,000	31,623	5,000	22,360
CHANNEL		3,286	11,952	2,786	8,452	4,929	21,958	4,179	15,526	6,571	33,806	5,071	23,905
"L" SHAPE		3,400	14,142	2,900	10,000	5,100	25,980	4,350	18,371	6,800	40,000	5,800	28,284
RECTANGLE		3,667	18,257	3,167	12,910	5,500	33,541	4,750	23,717	7,334	51,640	6,334	36,575
CYLINDER		3,000	17,800	2,500	12,615	4,500	32,776	3,750	25,176	6,000	50,462	5,000	35,002
DOME		2,000	11,896			3,000	21,850			4,000	33,642		

* EXTERIOR AREA DOES NOT INCLUDE SURFACE AREA ON GRADE. ROOF IS CONSIDERED TO BE FLAT.

THE ENERGY CHARACTER-
ISTICS OF EACH FORM WILL VARY
ACCORDING TO ITS ORIENTATION.
IN THE FOLLOWING PAGES, THE
GENERIC FORMS ARE STUDIED
IN TERMS OF THEIR INTERAC-
TION WITH THE SUN AND THE
RESULTING HEAT GAIN OR LOSS.
IT SHOULD BE NOTED THAT THE
RESULTS WILL VARY A FEW
PERCENTAGE POINTS AS LATI-
TUDES CHANGE. THEREFORE,
THE USER SHOULD VIEW THIS
TYPE OF ANALYSIS AS A PILOT
TO THE ACTUAL DESIGN ANAL-
YSIS. IN FIG. 4.18,"A" AND"B",
THE NORTH SIDE REMAINS IN
THE SHADE AT ALL TIMES.
FIG. 4.19. THIS ORIENTATION
ALLOWS ALL SIDES TO RECEIVE
SUNSHINE DURING THE DAY.

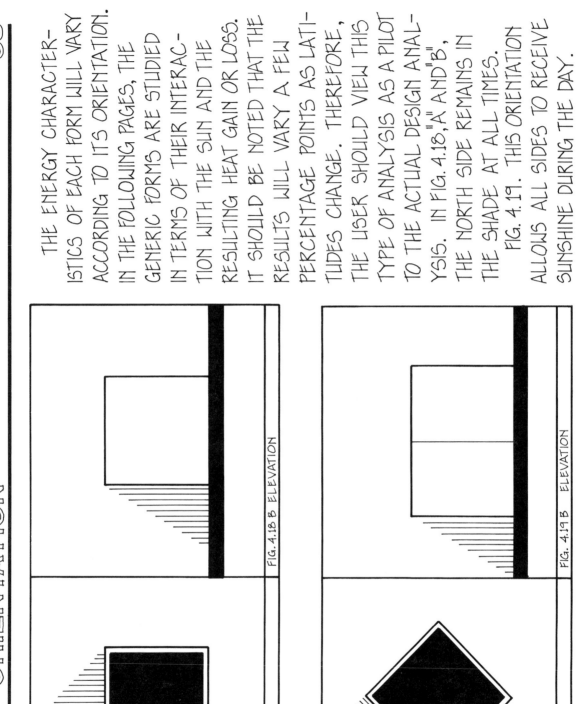

FIG. 4.18 B ELEVATION

FIG. 4.18 A PLAN

FIG. 4.19 B ELEVATION

FIG. 4.19 PLAN

FIGS. 4.19,
"A" AND "B", SHOW HOW WITH
THE USE OF CORRECT PROPOR-
TIONS, THE INTERIOR COURT
COULD BE MAINTAINED IN
SHADE THROUGHOUT THE DAY.
FOR AN ANALYSIS OF THE
SUN'S EFFECTS ON THE EXTE-
RIOR SURFACE, SEE THE
CUBE STUDY.

FIGS. 4.20, "A" AND "B",
ILLUSTRATE HOW THE OPPO-
SITE RESULT CAN BE ACHIEV-
ED THROUGH A SIMPLE
CHANGE IN THE ORIENTATION
OF THE GENERIC FORMS.

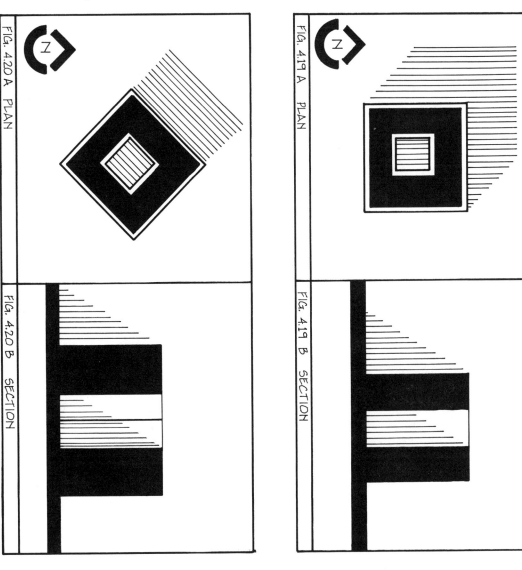

FIG. 4.20 A   PLAN

FIG. 4.20 B   SECTION

FIG. 4.19 A   PLAN

FIG. 4.19 B   SECTION

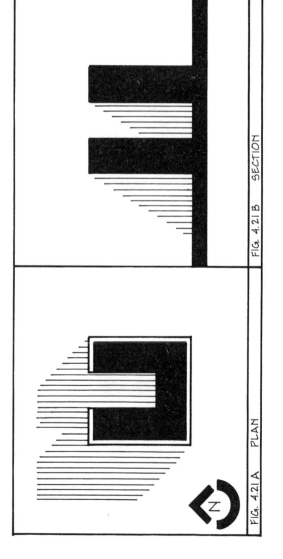

FIG. 4.21 A   PLAN

FIG. 4.21 B   SECTION

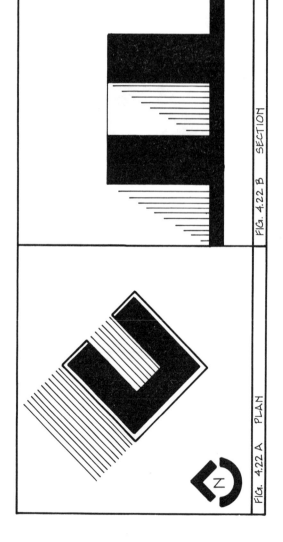

FIG. 4.22 A   PLAN

FIG. 4.22 B   SECTION

IN FIGS. 4.21, "A" AND "B",
THE ORIENTATION MAINTAINS
THE NORTHERN INTERIOR SIDE
IN THE SHADE. IN FIGS. 4.22,
"A" AND "B", THE ORIENTATION
EXPOSES ALL OF THE SIDES
TO THE SUN DURING THE DAY.

IN FIGS. 4.23, "A" AND "B", THE ORIENTATION MAINTAINS THE NORTHERN EXTERIOR SIDE IN THE SHADE, WHILE CREATING A HEAT TRAP. THIS FORM AND ORIENTATION WILL DECREASE THE HEATING LOAD.

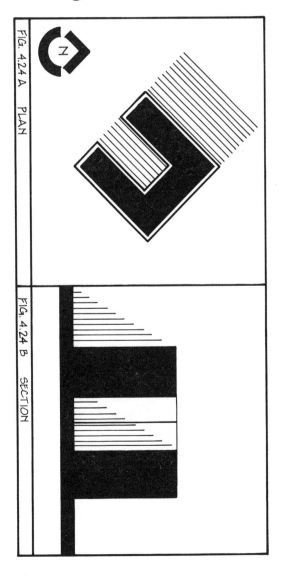

FIG. 4.24 A   PLAN

FIG. 4.24 B   SECTION

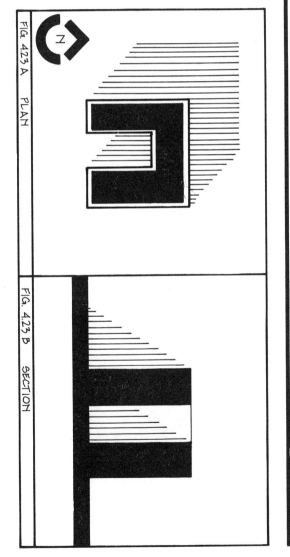

FIG. 4.23 A   PLAN

FIG. 4.23 B   SECTION

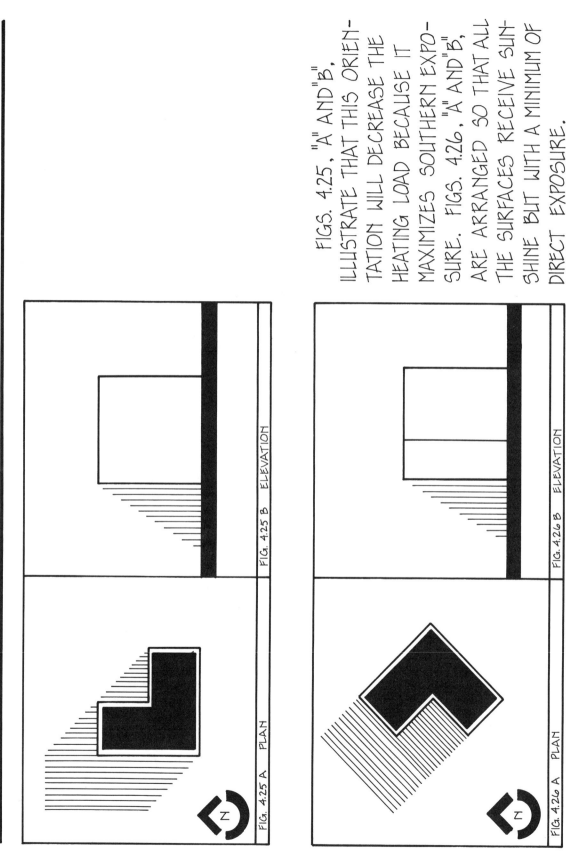

FIGS. 4.25, "A" AND "B",
ILLUSTRATE THAT THIS ORIEN-
TATION WILL DECREASE THE
HEATING LOAD BECAUSE IT
MAXIMIZES SOUTHERN EXPO-
SURE. FIGS. 4.26, "A" AND "B",
ARE ARRANGED SO THAT ALL
THE SURFACES RECEIVE SUN-
SHINE BUT WITH A MINIMUM OF
DIRECT EXPOSURE.

FIG. 4.25 B   ELEVATION

FIG. 4.25 A   PLAN

FIG. 4.26 B   ELEVATION

FIG. 4.26 A   PLAN

WITH THE ORIENTATION
SHOWN IN FIG. 4.27, SUN EXPO-
SURE IS MINIMIZED, THEREFORE
THE COOLING LOAD WILL BE
REDUCED. WITH THE ORIENTA-
TION SHOWN IN FIGS. 4.28, "A"
AND "B", THE WESTERN SIDE
ACTS AS A HEAT TRAP. THIS
CAN BE USED TO REDUCE
THE HEATING LOAD.

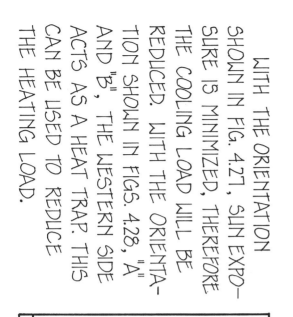

FIG. 4.28 A   PLAN

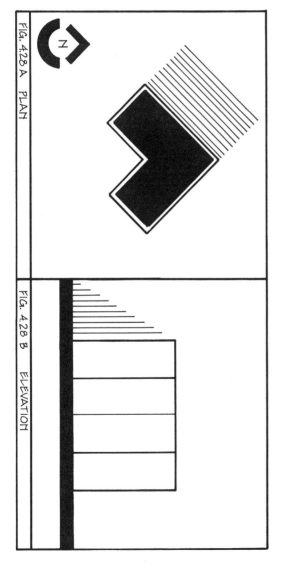

FIG. 4.28 B   ELEVATION

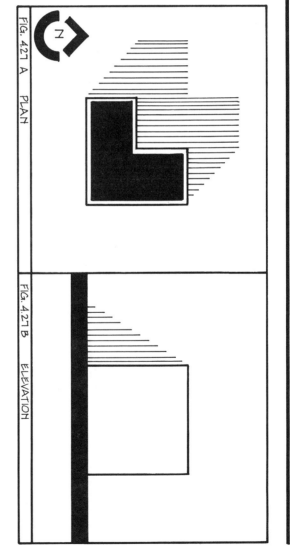

FIG. 4.27 A   PLAN

FIG. 4.27 B   ELEVATION

FIGS. 4.29, "A" AND "B", SHOW THE TYPE OF ORIENTATION WHICH MAXIMIZES THE SOUTHERN EXPOSURE AND MAINTAINS THE NORTH SIDE IN SHADE.

FIGS. 4.30, "A" AND "B", ILLUSTRATE THE ORIENTATION WHICH MINIMIZES SOUTHERN EXPOSURE.

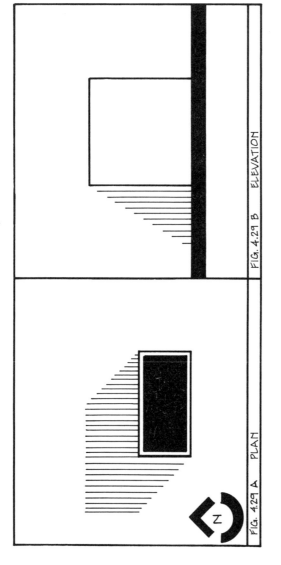

FIG. 4.29 A   PLAN

FIG. 4.29 B   ELEVATION

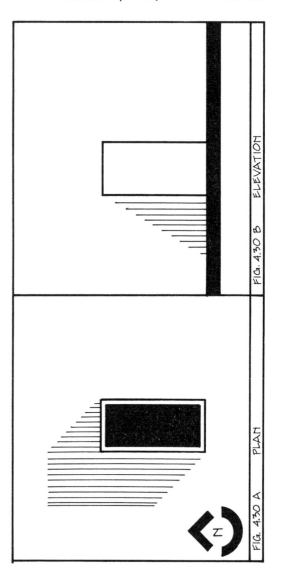

FIG. 4.30 A   PLAN

FIG. 4.30 B   ELEVATION

FIGS. 4.30, "C"–"F", DEPICT THAT THE ORIENTATION IS NOT A MAJOR CONSIDERATION FOR THESE SPECIFIC FORMS.

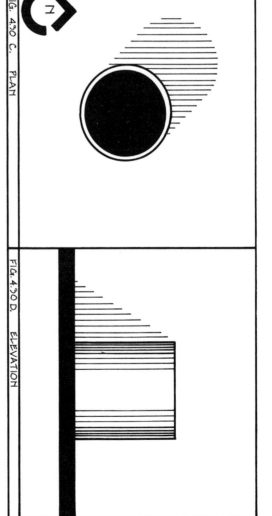

FIG. 4:30 C.   PLAN

FIG. 4:30 D.   ELEVATION

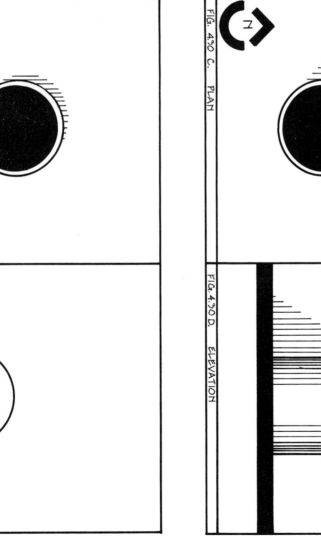

FIG. 4:30 E.   PLAN

FIG. 4:30 F.   ELEVATION

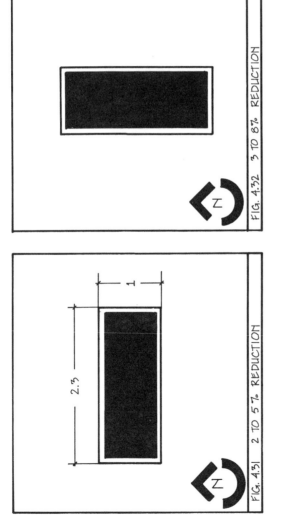

FIG. 4.31　2 TO 5% REDUCTION

FIG. 4.32　3 TO 8% REDUCTION

FIG. 4.33　5 TO 9% REDUCTION

FIG. 4.34　6 TO 8% REDUCTION

FIGS. 4.31 THROUGH 4.34 ILLUSTRATE THE AVERAGE REDUCTION IN HEATING LOADS FOR THE 40° LATITUDE. ALL THE FORMS HAVE EQUAL FLOOR AREAS. [18]

FIGS. 4.35 THROUGH 4.38
SHOW THE PREFERRED FORMS
AND THEIR PROPORTIONS FOR
THE PARTICULAR CLIMATIC
REGIONS. THEIR CHOICE WAS
BASED ON THE BALANCE
THEY CREATE IN THE UNDER
HEATED AND OVERHEATED
SEASONS. IT IS IMPORTANT
TO NOTE THAT ALL PREFER-
RED SHAPES ARE ELONGA-
TED ON THE EAST-WEST
AXIS. OPTIMUM DIMENSIONS
ARE REPRESENTED BY THE
SHADED AREAS, GOOD DI-
MENSIONS BY THE WHITE
AREAS. [19]

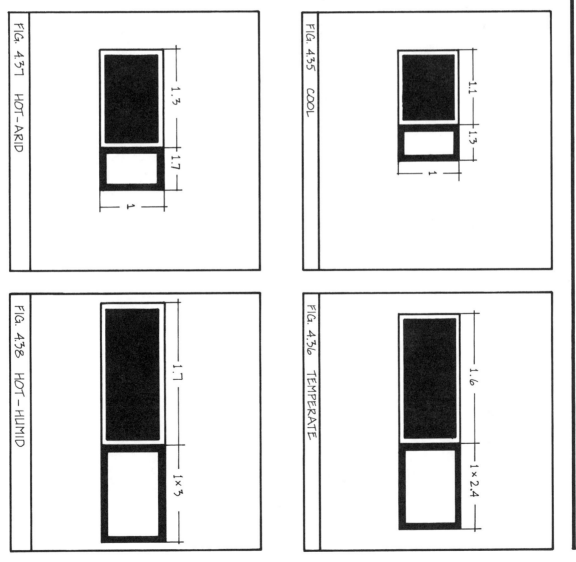

FIG. 4.35   COOL

FIG. 4.36   TEMPERATE

FIG. 4.37   HOT-ARID

FIG. 4.38   HOT-HUMID

THE EARTH'S SURFACE FRIC-
TION SLOWS THE WIND FLOW.
NATURAL AND MAN-MADE BAR-
RIERS ALTER WIND FLOW PAT-
TERN AND SPEED. WIND VELO-
CITY IS REPRESENTED AS A
PERCENTAGE OF THE OPEN
FIELD VELOCITY. FIGS. 4.40
AND 4.41 DEPICT HOW THE
AREAS AT THE END OF THE
WALL ARE SUBJECT TO HIGH-
ER WIND VELOCITIES.

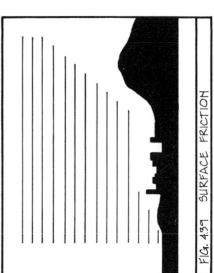

FIG. 4.39   SURFACE FRICTION

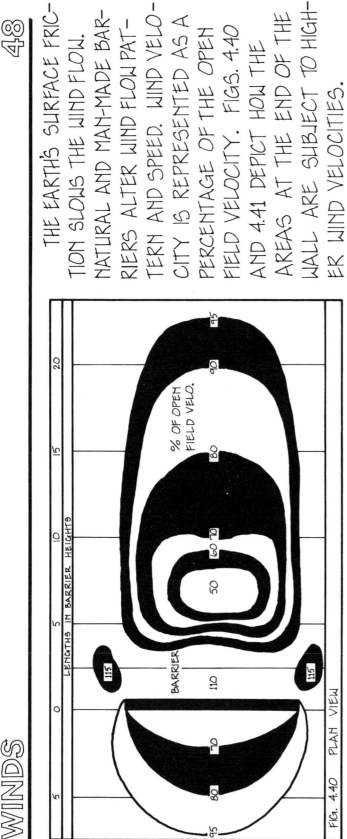

% OF OPEN
FIELD VELO.

LENGTHS IN BARRIER HEIGHTS

FIG. 4.40   PLAN VIEW

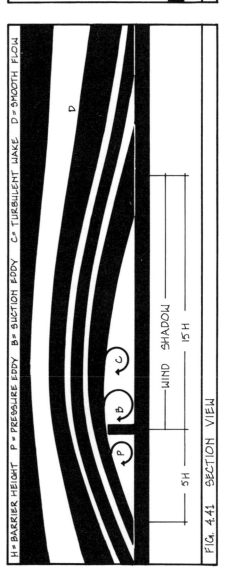

H = BARRIER HEIGHT   P = PRESSURE EDDY   B = SUCTION EDDY   C = TURBULENT WAKE   D = SMOOTH FLOW

WIND SHADOW

FIG. 4.41   SECTION VIEW

THE PATH WINDS FOLLOW OVER NATURAL OR MAN-MADE OBJECTS IS A PRODUCT OF THE SHAPES AND DIMENSIONS OF THE OBSTACLES. FIGS. 4.42 THROUGH 4.47 PRESENT THE TERMINOLOGY USED TO IDENTIFY THE EFFECTS AND CHARACTERISTICS OF WIND FLOW.

FIG. 4.42 PATTERNS ELEVATION

FIG. 4.44 EDDIES ELEVATION

HIGH

LOW

FIG. 4.46 PRESSURES ELEVATION

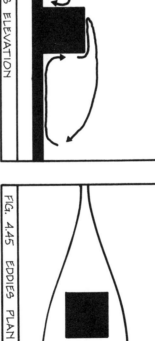

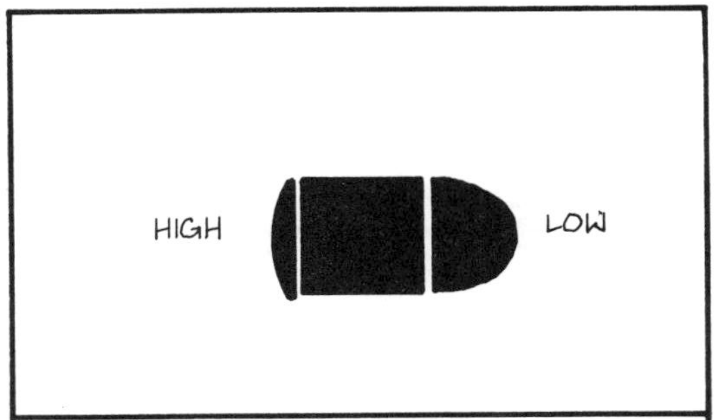

FIG. 4.43 PATTERNS PLAN

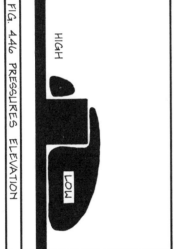

FIG. 4.45 EDDIES PLAN

HIGH

LOW

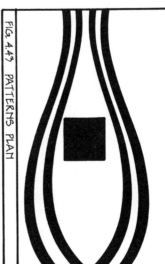

FIG. 4.47 PRESSURES PLAN

WIND PATTERNS

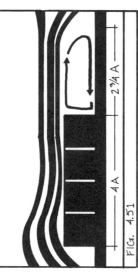

FIG. 4.51
4 A
2¾ A

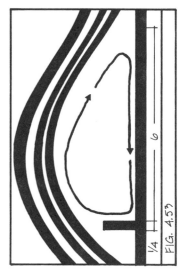

FIG. 4.52
1½
4½ A

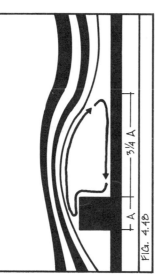

FIG. 4.48
1 A
3¾ A

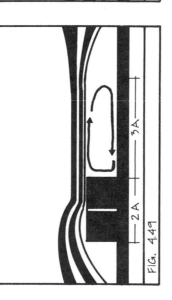

FIG. 4.49
2 A
3 A

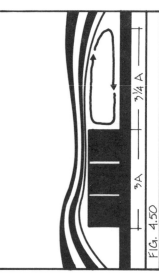

FIG. 4.50
3 A
3¼ A

1/4
FIG. 4.53
6

FIGS. 4.48 THROUGH 4.53 SHOW THE RESULTING WIND PATTERNS WHEN THE DEPTH OF THE FLAT-TOP BUILDING VARIES.

WIND PATTERNS

OVERHANGS INCREASE
THE UPWIND EDDY AREA.

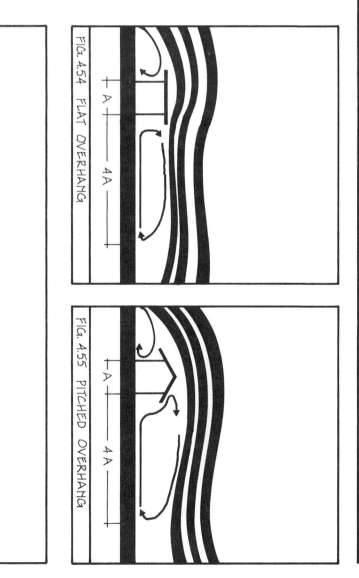

FIG. 4.54   FLAT OVERHANG

FIG. 4.55   PITCHED OVERHANG

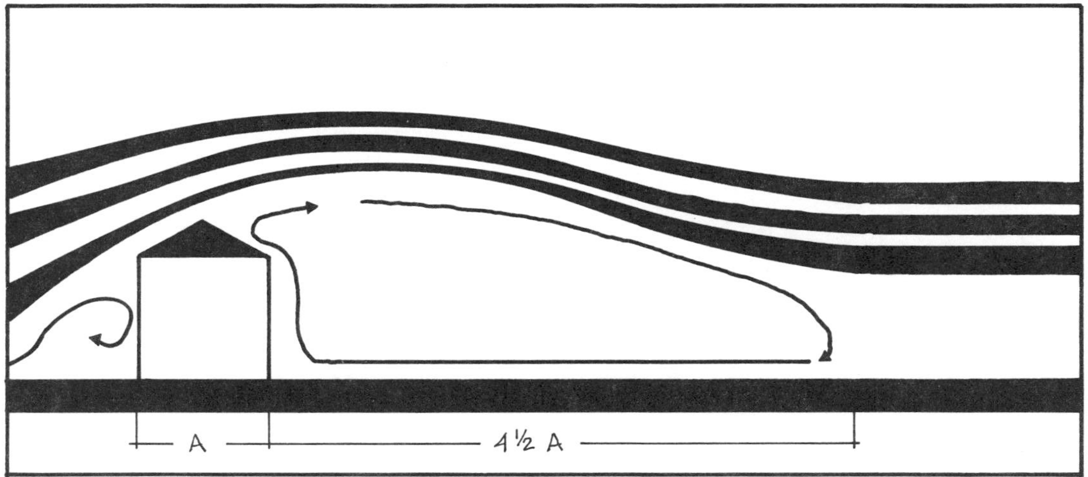

FIG. 4.56   PITCHED ROOF

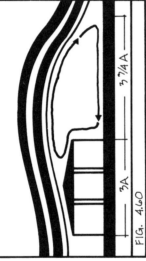

FIG. 4.57

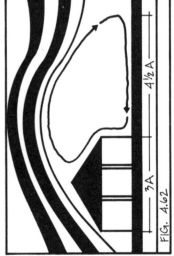

3 ¾ A

FIG. 4.60

3 A

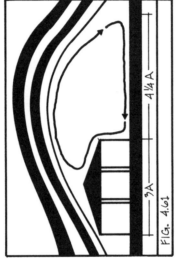

FIG. 4.58

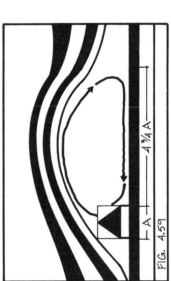

4 ¼ A

FIG. 4.61

3 A

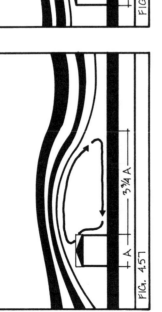

FIG. 4.59

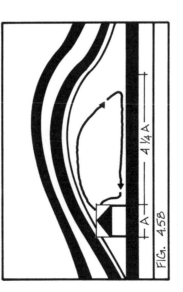

4 ½ A

FIG. 4.62

3 A

THE EDDY CHARACTERIS-
TICS ARE AFFECTED BY
THE ROOF PITCH. AS IT IN-
CREASES, SO DOES THE
HEIGHT AND DEPTH OF THE
EDDY.

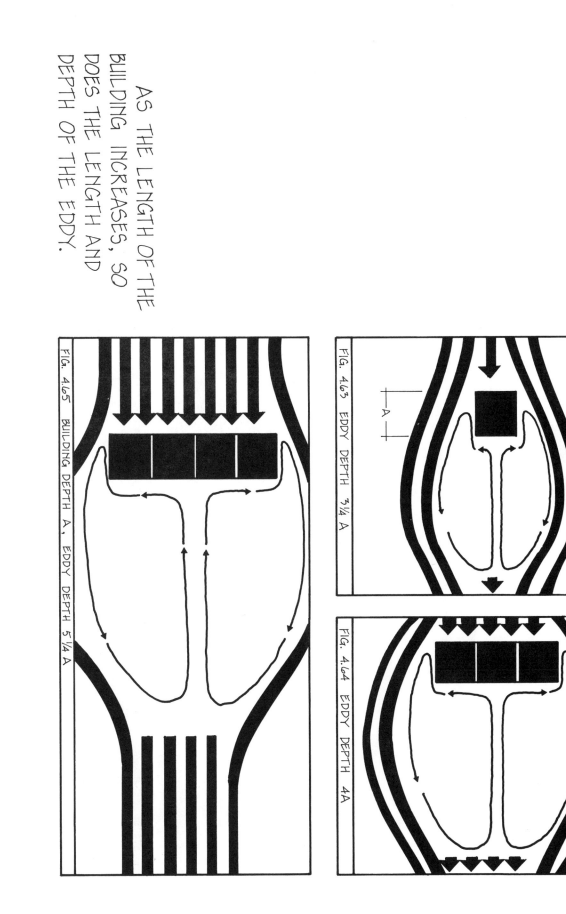

WIND PATTERNS

AS THE LENGTH OF THE BUILDING INCREASES, SO DOES THE LENGTH AND DEPTH OF THE EDDY.

FIG. 4.63 EDDY DEPTH 3/4 A

A

FIG. 4.64 EDDY DEPTH 4A

FIG. 4.65 BUILDING DEPTH A, EDDY DEPTH 5 1/4 A

WIND PATTERNS

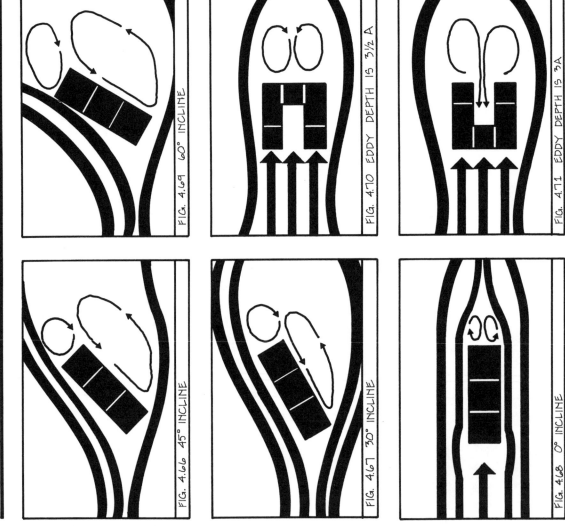

FIG. 4.66 45° INCLINE

FIG. 4.67 30° INCLINE

FIG. 4.68 0° INCLINE

FIG. 4.69 60° INCLINE

FIG. 4.70 EDDY DEPTH IS 3½ A

FIG. 4.71 EDDY DEPTH IS 3A

EDDY CHARACTERISTICS ARE AFFECTED BY BUILDING ORIENTATION.

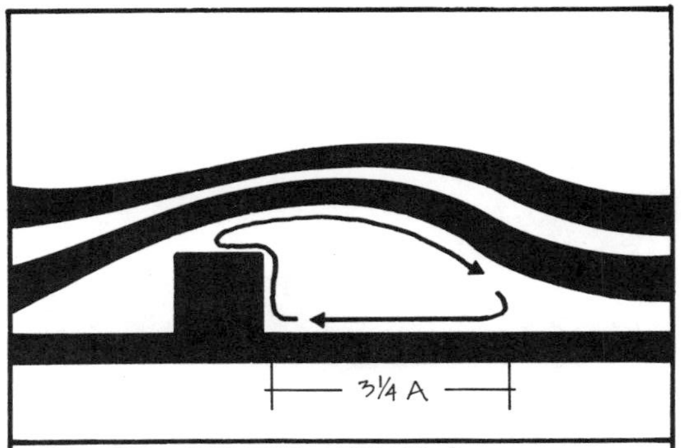

VARIATIONS IN THE HEIGHT
OF THE OBJECT CAUSE AN
INCREASE IN THE AMOUNT OF
AIR FLOWING AROUND IT. THE
AMOUNT OF AIR MOVING
OVER THE OBJECT REMAINS
CONSTANT.

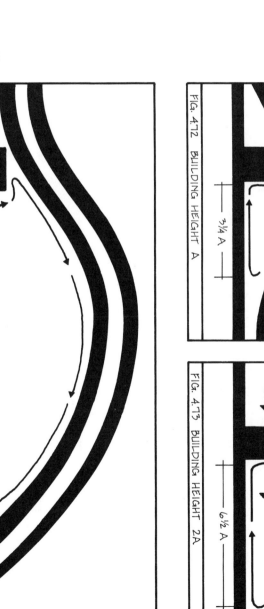

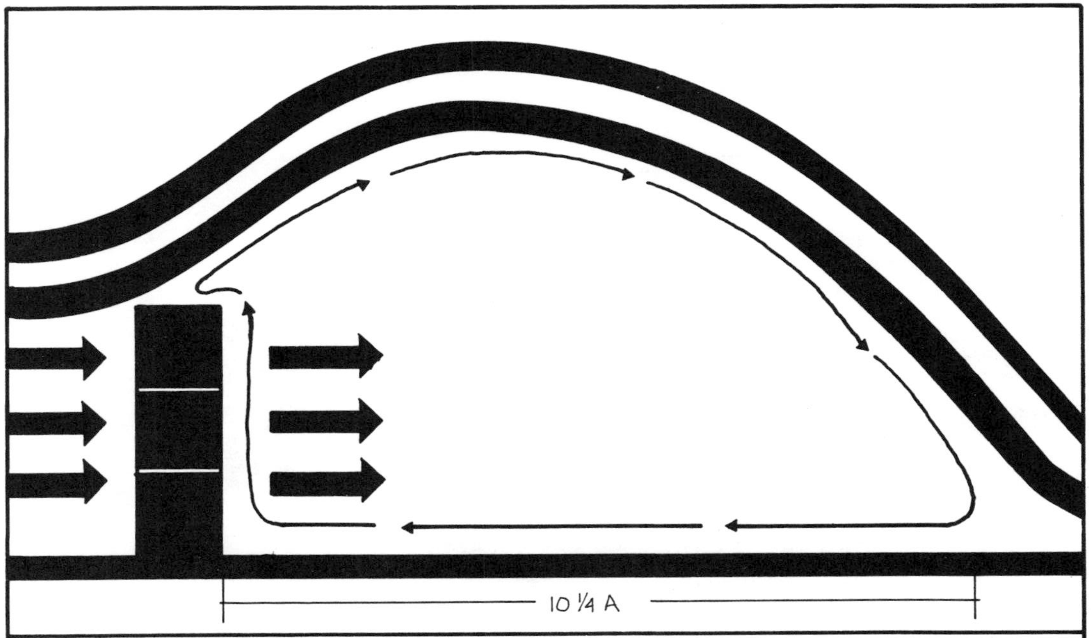

FIG. 4.72 BUILDING HEIGHT A

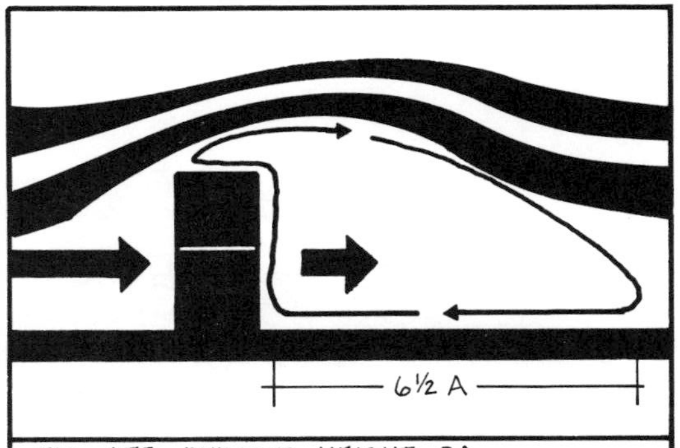

¾ A

FIG. 4.73 BUILDING HEIGHT 2A

6½ A

FIG. 4.74 BUILDING HEIGHT 3A

10¼ A

WHEN A WIND CURRENT FLOWS OVER AN OBSTACLE, IT CHANGES INTO A TURBULENT FLOW. THIS SIMPLY MEANS THAT INSTEAD OF IT MOVING IN A STRAIGHT, FORWARD DIRECTION, IT TENDS TO ROTATE AS IT CONTINUES ITS PATH. THIS ROTATING MOTION INCREASES THE WIND'S HEAT EXTRACTION CHARACTERISTICS. THIS TRAIT CAN BE MANIPULATED TO INCREASE OR DECREASE THE BUILDING'S COOLING LOADS.

FIGS. 4.75 AND 4.76 SHOW HOW THE ROTATING MOTION OF THE WIND ALLOWS A LARGE AIR FLOW OVER THE BUILDING'S SURFACE.

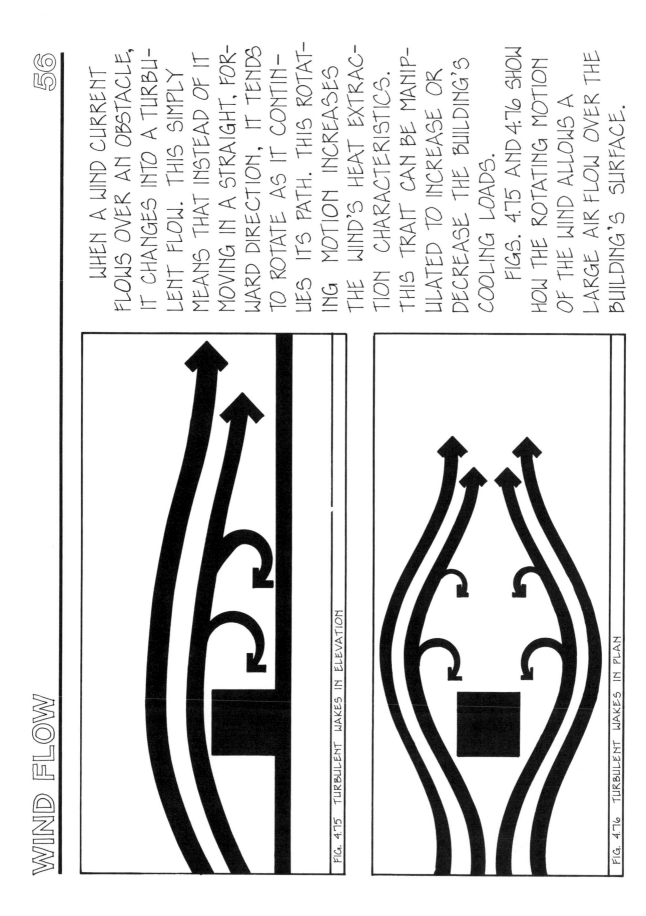

FIG. 4.75 TURBULENT WAKES IN ELEVATION

FIG. 4.76 TURBULENT WAKES IN PLAN

DEPENDING ON THE TYPE OF SURFACE, HEAT AND LIGHT WILL BE ABSORBED OR REFLECTED. THESE CHARACTERISTICS SHOULD BE STUDIED WHEN ANALYZING POSSIBLE LOCATIONS FOR ACCESS ROADS. FOR EXAMPLE, IF A ROAD IS TAR PAVED, IT SHOULD NOT BE PLACED IN THE PATH OF SUMMER BREEZES BECAUSE THE WIND WILL ABSORB THE HEAT FROM THE ROAD AND THEREBY REDUCE ITS COOLING POTENTIAL. A BETTER SOLUTION WOULD BE TO PLACE THE ROAD IN THE WINTER WIND PATH. THIS ALLOWS THE WIND TO ABSORB SOME OF THE ROAD'S HEAT AND EFFECTIVELY REDUCE ITS COOLING CAPACITY.

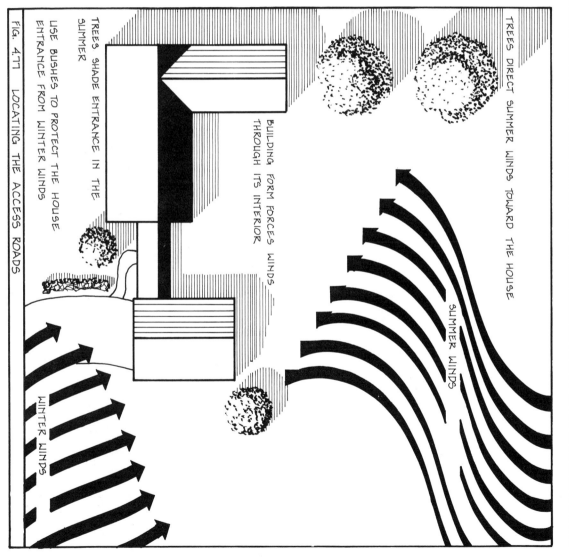

TREES DIRECT SUMMER WINDS TOWARD THE HOUSE

SUMMER WINDS

BUILDING FORM FORCES WINDS THROUGH ITS INTERIOR

TREES SHADE ENTRANCE IN THE SUMMER

USE BUSHES TO PROTECT THE HOUSE ENTRANCE FROM WINTER WINDS

WINTER WINDS

FIG. 4.77 LOCATING THE ACCESS ROADS

BERMS CAN BE USED TO INCREASE INSULATION, TO REDUCE HEAT LOSSES AND GAINS, TO PROTECT THE BUILDING FROM WINDS AND TO CHANNEL AWAY WATER FROM THE EXTERIOR SURFACES.

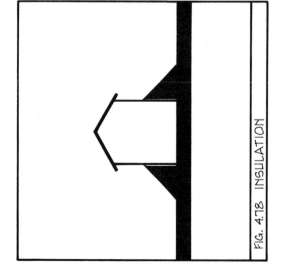

FIG. 4.78 INSULATION

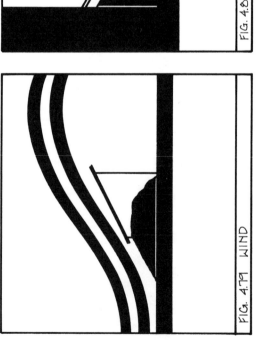

FIG. 4.79 WIND

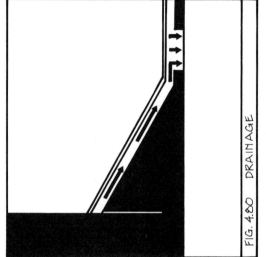

FIG. 4.80 DRAINAGE

GROUND WATER

THE MOISTURE CONTENT
IN SIMILAR TYPES OF SOIL
IS INFLUENCED BY THE BED-
ROCK STRUCTURE; FIG. 4.81
SHOWS WATER DRAINING IN-
TO THE BEDROCK. FIG. 4.82
SHOWS WATER DRAINING
THROUGH THE BEDROCK. ON
GENTLY DISSECTED BED-
ROCK, WATER COLLECTS
IN SHALLOW CREVICES,
FIG. 4.83, OR IT MOVES IN
A PLANE DOWN THE SLOPE,
FIG. 4.84. THESE CHARAC-
TERISTICS SHOULD BE
STUDIED PRIOR TO THE
BUILDING DESIGN SINCE
THEY AFFECT THE THERMAL
VALUES OF THE SITE.

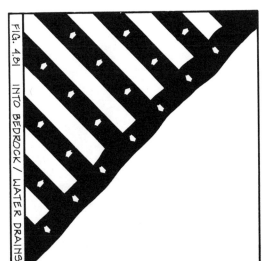

FIG. 4.81 INTO BEDROCK / WATER DRAINS

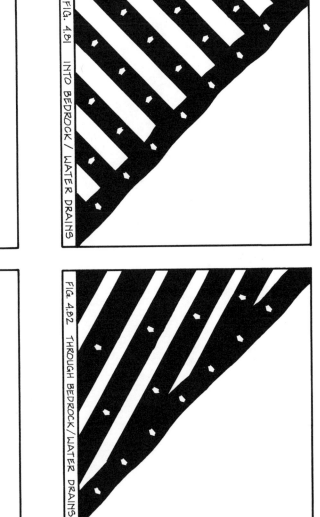

FIG. 4.82 THROUGH BEDROCK/WATER DRAINS

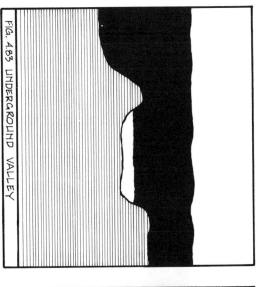

FIG. 4.83 UNDERGROUND VALLEY

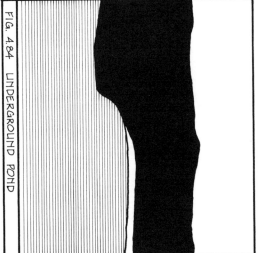

FIG. 4.84 UNDERGROUND POND

IT IS POSSIBLE TO USE
ARTIFICIAL PONDS AND
FOUNTAINS, IN ADDITION
TO NATURAL BODIES OF
WATER, AROUND THE BUILD-
ING TO REDUCE THE EXTE-
RIOR AIR TEMPERATURES.
IT IS ALSO POSSIBLE TO
PLACE THESE WATER BOD-
IES IN THE PATH OF SUM-
MER WINDS IN ORDER TO
FURTHER COOL THE WIND
CURRENTS.

COOL AIR

WARM AIR

FIG. 4.85 DAYTIME HEAT ABSORPTION

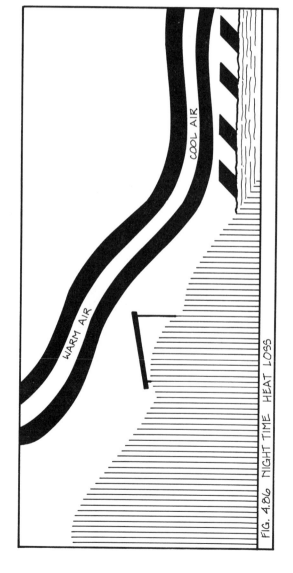

WARM AIR

COOL AIR

FIG. 4.86 NIGHT TIME HEAT LOSS

FLAT ROOFS TEND TO CRE-
ATE SMALL WATER PONDS.
WHEN PROPERLY CONTROL-
LED, THIS CONDITION COULD
BE USED TO DECREASE THE
COOLING LOAD; FIG. 4.87.
LOW PITCHED ROOFS ALLOW
SNOW AND ICE TO ACCUMU-
LATE ON THEM. THIS TENDS
TO DECREASE THE HEATING
LOADS; FIG. 4.88.

STEEPLY SLOPED ROOFS
PERMIT THE SNOW TO SLIDE
OFF; FIG. 4.89. WATER IN
IT'S VAPOROUS STAGE CAN
ACCUMULATE UNDER OVER-
HANGS AND SCREENS. THE
DESIGNER SHOULD STUDY
THESE POSSIBILITIES TO IN-
SURE THAT NO DETRIMEN-
TAL EFFECTS ARE CAUSED.

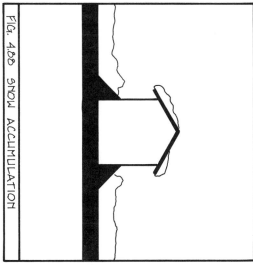

FIG. 4.88 SNOW ACCUMULATION

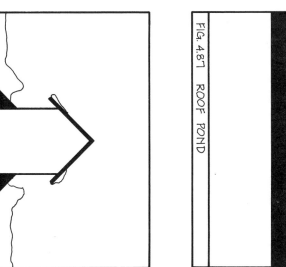

FIG. 4.89 MINIMAL SNOW ACCUMULATION

FIG. 4.87 ROOF POND

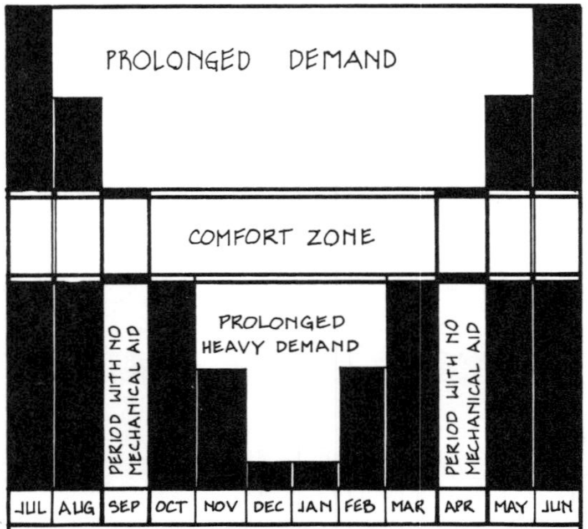

THE HUMAN COMFORT ZONE IS DEFINED AS THE RANGE IN THE INTERACTION OF AIR TEMPERATURES AND THE LEVELS OF HUMIDITY AND AIR MOVEMENT WHICH COMBINE TO CREATE A PLEASANT AND HEALTHY ATMOSPHERE FOR THE BUILDING'S INHABITANTS. MAN HAS DESIGNED MECHANICAL SYSTEMS IN ORDER TO ACHIEVE AND MAINTAIN THESE THERMALLY COMFORTABLE ENVIRONMENTS. FIG. 5.1 ILLUSTRATES, BY USE OF HISTOGRAMS, THE INTERIOR CLIMATIC VARIATIONS THAT WOULD TAKE PLACE IN A TYPICAL BUILDING IF THESE MECHANICAL SYSTEMS WERE NOT OPERATING. FIG. 5.2, ON THE OTHER HAND, ILLUSTRATES THE INTERIOR CLIMATIC VARIATIONS OF AN ENERGY CONSCIOUS BUILDING WITH ITS SYSTEMS NONOPERATIVE. THE ENERGY CONSCIOUS BUILDING HAS LESS CLIMATIC VARIATIONS AND THEREFORE IT CONSUMES MUCH LESS ENERGY. IT HAS BEEN ESTIMATED THAT ENERGY CONSCIOUS DESIGN CAN REDUCE THE ENERGY CONSUMPTION OF A BUILDING BY 40% OR MORE.

PROLONGED DEMAND

COMFORT ZONE

PROLONGED HEAVY DEMAND

PERIOD WITH NO MECHANICAL AID

PERIOD WITH NO MECHANICAL AID

JUL AUG SEP OCT NOV DEC JAN FEB MAR APR MAY JUN

FIG. 5.1 TYPICAL DESIGN

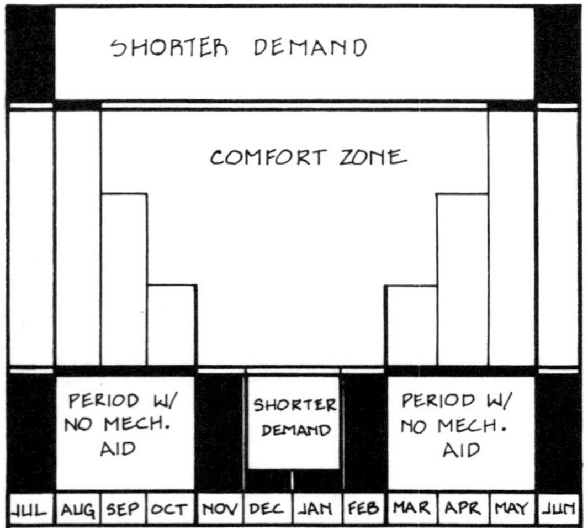

SHORTER DEMAND

COMFORT ZONE

PERIOD W/ NO MECH. AID

SHORTER DEMAND

PERIOD W/ NO MECH. AID

JUL AUG SEP OCT NOV DEC JAN FEB MAR APR MAY JUN

FIG. 5.2 ENERGY CONSCIOUS DESIGN

TEMPERATURE AND HUMIDITY

RELATIVE HUMIDITY IN PER-
CENTAGE IS THE AMOUNT OF
WATER VAPOR IN THE AIR COM-
PARED TO THE MAXIMUM
AMOUNT THAT COULD BE CON-
TAINED IN THE SAME VOLUME
AT THAT SPECIFIC TEMPERA-
TURE. THE INTERACTION OF
AIR TEMPERATURE AND
RELATIVE HUMIDITY IS
ILLUSTRATED IN FIG. 5.3.
HUMAN BEINGS HAVE A
HIGHER TOLERANCE TO
HUMIDITY IN THE COMFORT
ZONE THAN TO HIGH
TEMPERATURES.[20]

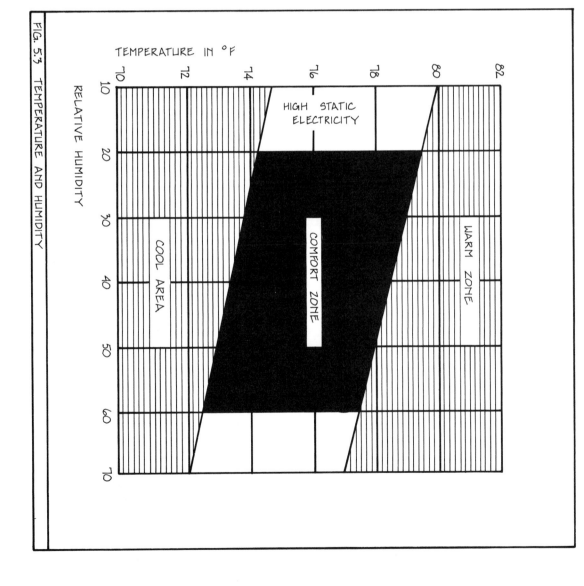

FIG. 5.3   TEMPERATURE AND HUMIDITY

FIGS. 5.4 THROUGH 5.7
LIST THE AMOUNT OF
BTUH'S RELEASED BY A
PERSON ENGAGED IN DIFFER-
ENT ACTIVITIES. THESE
QUANTITIES SHOULD BE IN-
CLUDED WHEN CALCULAT-
ING COOLING LOADS.[21]

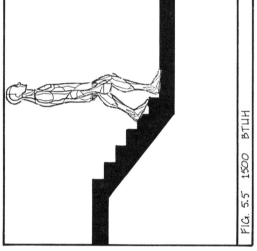

FIG. 5.4   4400 BTUH

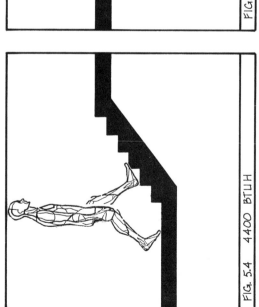

FIG. 5.5   1500 BTUH

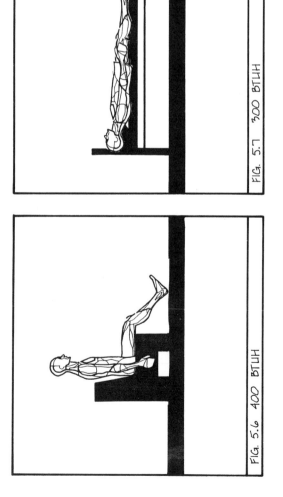

FIG. 5.6   400 BTUH

FIG. 5.7   300 BTUH

HEAT FROM APPLIANCES

FIGS. 5.8 THROUGH 5.11
LIST THE AMOUNT OF BTUH's
RELEASED BY DOMESTIC
APPLIANCES. [22]

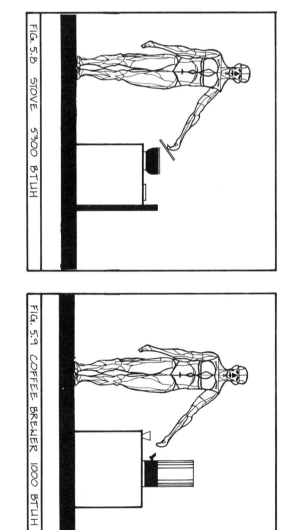

FIG. 5.8 STOVE 5300 BTUH

FIG. 5.9 COFFEE BREWER 1000 BTUH

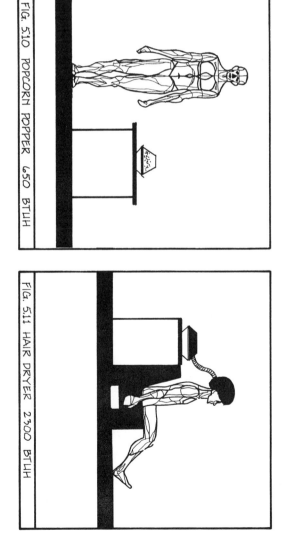

FIG. 5.10 POPCORN POPPER 650 BTUH

FIG. 5.11 HAIR DRYER 2300 BTUH

AIR VELOCITIES AND TEMPERATURES MUST BE CAREFULLY CONTROLLED SINCE THEY CAN PRODUCE COOLING BREEZES AND UNCOMFORTABLE DRAFTS. THE RANGE OF AIR VELO-CITY AND TEMPERATURES IS PRESENTED IN FIG. 5.12.[23]

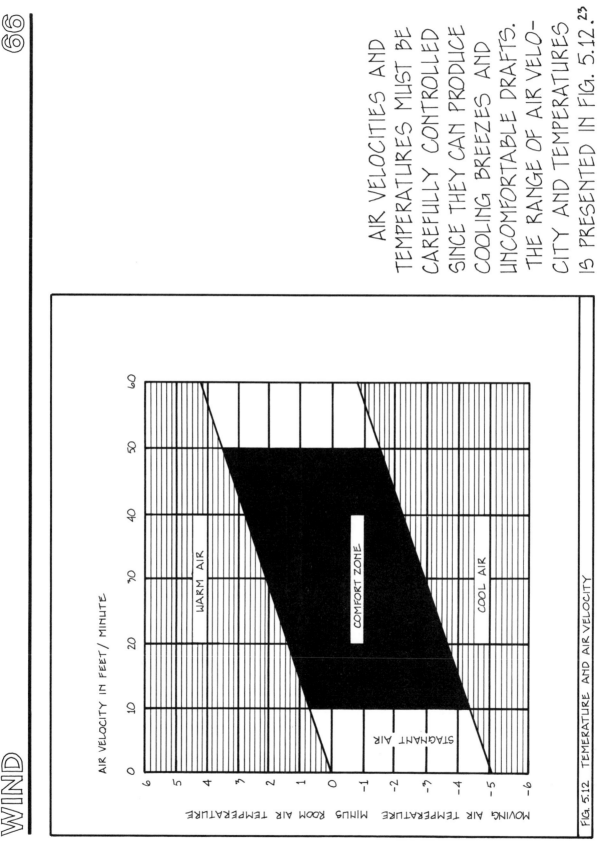

FIG. 5.12 TEMERATURE AND AIR VELOCITY

FIG. 5.13. TO CREATE AN INTERIOR AIR FLOW IT IS NECESSARY TO HAVE BOTH INLETS AND OUTLETS.

FIG. 5.14. A LARGE IN- LET WITH A SMALL OUTLET CREATES AIR FLOWS OF LOW SPEEDS IN THE BUILDING'S INTERIOR. THIS IS NOT EFFEC- TIVE FOR NATURAL COOLING.

FIG. 5.15. A SMALL INLET WITH A LARGE OUTLET CRE- ATES HIGH SPEEDS IN THE INTERIOR. THIS IS MORE EFFECTIVE NATURAL COOLING.

FIG. 5.16. A LARGE INLET WITH A LARGE OUTLET OPPO- SITE IT CREATES MAXIMUM AIR FLOW. THIS IS A PRE- FERRED CODITION FOR NATURAL COOLING.

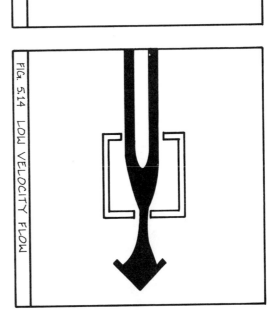

FIG. 5.13 NO AIR FLOW

FIG. 5.14 LOW VELOCITY FLOW

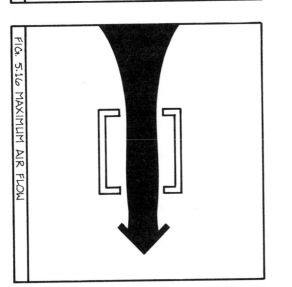

FIG. 5.15 HIGH VELOCITY FLOW

FIG. 5.16 MAXIMUM AIR FLOW

FIG. 5.17. OFFSETTING THE INLET AND OUTLET CAUSES THE AIR TO FLOW AT AN ANGLE.

FIG. 5.18. AN INLET WITH A LOUVER CAN BE USED TO DIRECT THE AIR FLOW.

FIGS. 5.19 AND 5.20. THESE ARRANGEMENTS OF THE INLETS AND OUTLETS CAUSES THE AIR TO FLOW AROUND THE INTERIOR WALLS. THE AIR FLOW IS CONSTANT REGARDLESS OF OBSTACLES PLACED OUTSIDE THE FLOW PATTERN.

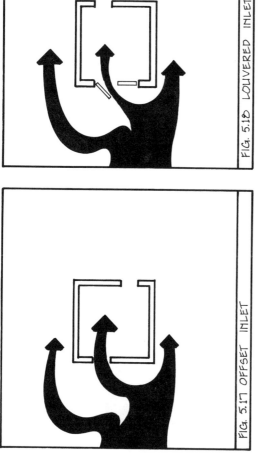

FIG. 5.17 OFFSET INLET

FIG. 5.18 LOUVERED INLET

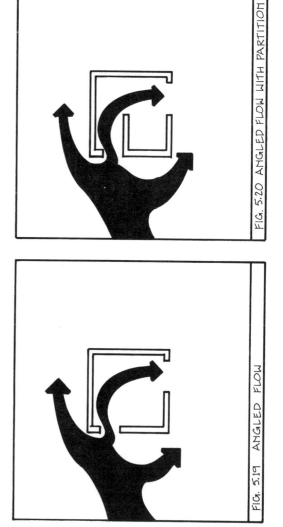

FIG. 5.19 ANGLED FLOW

FIG. 5.20 ANGLED FLOW WITH PARTITION

FIG. 5.21. THE AIR FLOW IS ALTERED AND THE SPEED REDUCED WHEN AN OBSTACLE IS PLACED IN THE ORIGINAL FLOW PATH.

FIG. 5.22. THE PLACEMENT OF AN OBSTACLE IN THIS POSITION REDUCES THE COOLING EFFECTIVENESS OF THE AIR CURRENT.

FIG. 5.23. OBSTACLES PLACED PARALLEL TO THE ORIGINAL AIR FLOW DIVIDE THE PATTERN BUT DO NOT REDUCE THE COOLING EFFICIENCY.

FIG. 5.24. OBSTACLES PERPENDICULAR TO THE ORIGINAL AIR FLOW REDUCE THE COOLING EFFICIENCY.

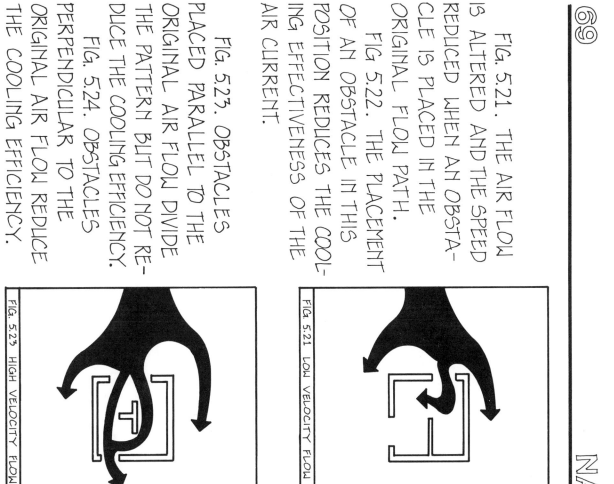

FIG. 5.21 LOW VELOCITY FLOW

FIG. 5.23 HIGH VELOCITY FLOW

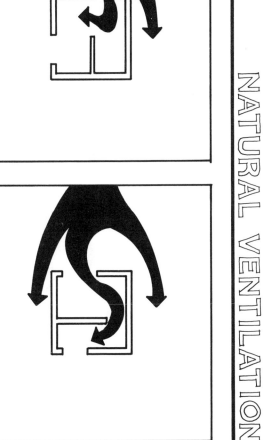

FIG. 5.22 LOW COOLING CAPACITY

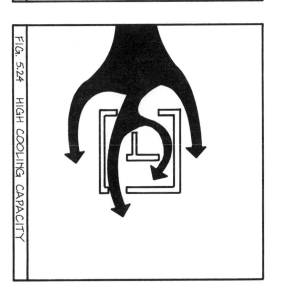

FIG. 5.24 HIGH COOLING CAPACITY

FIG. 5.25. INLETS AND OUTLETS LOCATED IN THE CENTER OF THE WALL CREATE AN AIR FLOW IN THE LIVING LEVELS.

FIG. 5.26. INLETS LOCATED IN THE BOTTOM OF THE WALL CREATE AN AIR FLOW THROUGH THE FLOOR LEVELS.

FIG. 5.27. LOW INLETS AND HIGH OUTLETS EFFECTIVELY RELEASE HOT AIR.

FIG. 5.28. LOW INLETS AND LOW OUTLETS CREATE AIR FLOW THROUGH FLOOR LEVELS WITHOUT REMOVING THE HOT AIR.

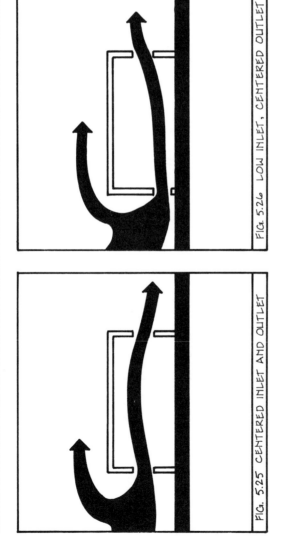

FIG. 5.25 CENTERED INLET AND OUTLET

FIG. 5.26 LOW INLET, CENTERED OUTLET

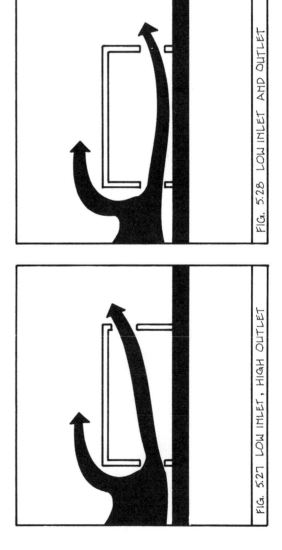

FIG. 5.27 LOW INLET, HIGH OUTLET

FIG. 5.28 LOW INLET AND OUTLET

FIG. 5.29. HIGH INLETS AND OUTLETS EFFECTIVELY RELEASE HOT AIR BUT DO NOT CREATE AN AIR FLOW THROUGH THE LIVING LEVELS.

FIG. 5.30. OVERHANGS COLLECT AIR STREAMS WHICH OTHERWISE WOULD TEND TO ESCAPE. THIS IMPROVES THE INTERIOR AIR FLOW.

FIG. 5.31. OVERHANGS AT TOP WINDOW LEVELS CREATE AN AIR FLOW THROUGH THE CEILING LEVELS.

FIG. 5.32. UNATTACHED OVERHANGS AT TOP WINDOW LEVELS CREATE AN AIR FLOW THROUGH THE LIVING LEVELS.

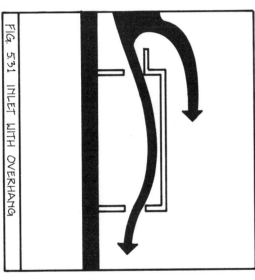

FIG. 5.31 INLET WITH OVERHANG

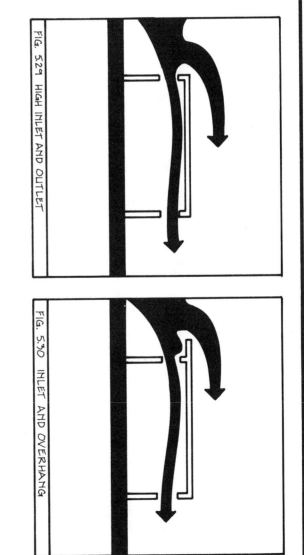

FIG. 5.29 HIGH INLET AND OUTLET

FIG. 5.30 INLET AND OVERHANG

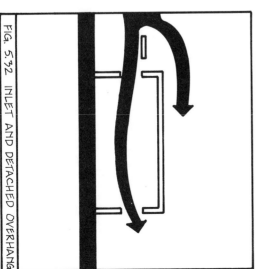

FIG. 5.32 INLET AND DETACHED OVERHANG

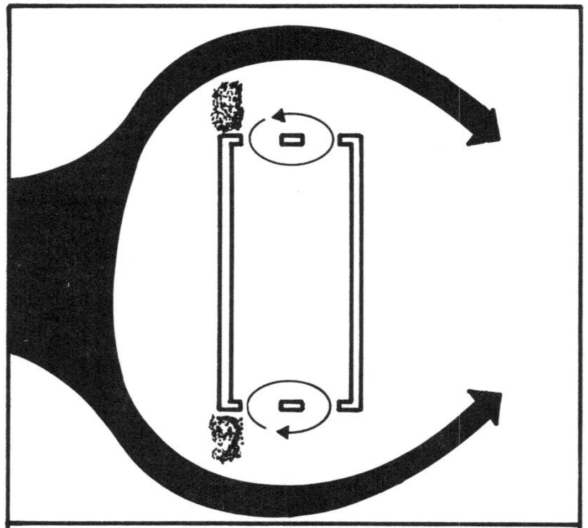

NATURAL VENTILATION

FIG. 5.33. HIGH OBSTA-
CLES LOCATED IN THE POSI-
TIONS SHOWN WILL MAINTAIN
THE ORIGINAL AIR FLOW
PATTERNS.

FIG. 5.34. MEDIUM HEIGHT
OR TALL OBSTACLES LO-
CATED IN THE POSITION
SHOWN WILL CREATE AN
AIR FLOW WITHIN THE
BUILDING.

FIG. 5.35. MEDIUM HEIGHT
OR TALL OBSTACLES LOCAT-
ED IN THE POSITIONS
SHOWN WILL CREATE AN AIR
FLOW THROUGH THE BUILD-
ING.

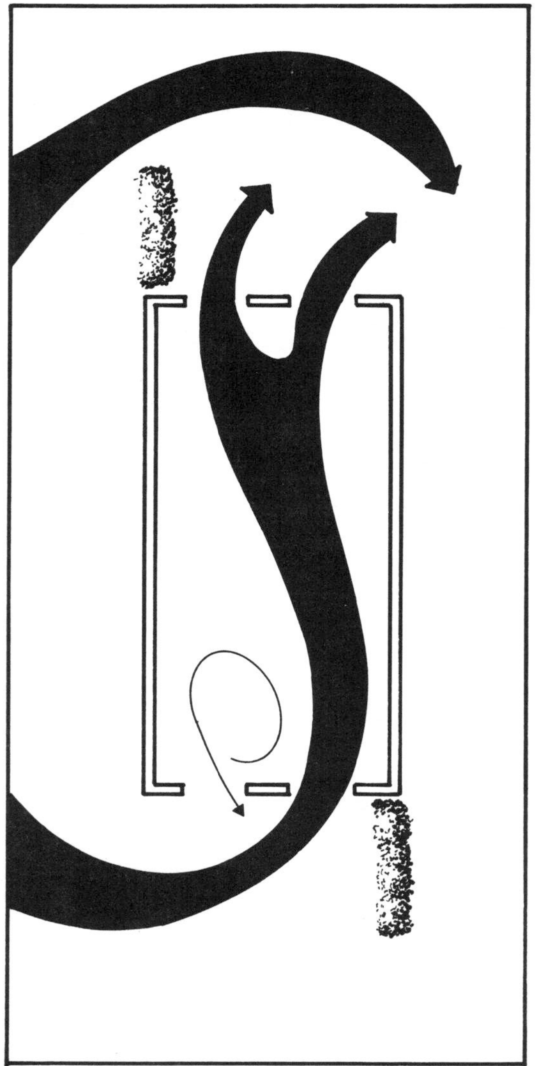

FIG. 5.35 VAST INTERIOR AIR FLOW

FIG. 5.33 NO INTERIOR AIR FLOW

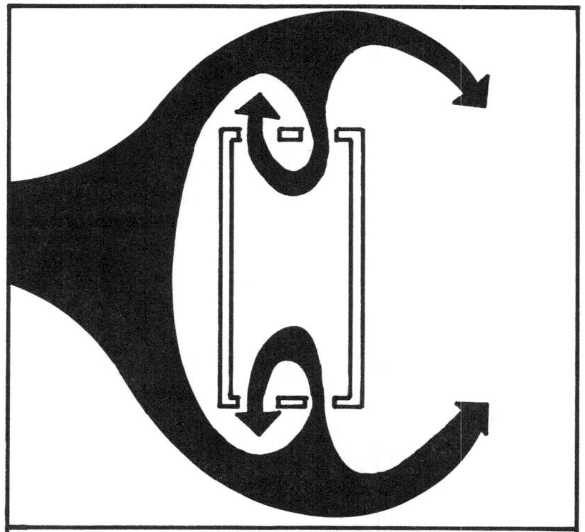

FIG. 5.34 LIMITED INTERIOR AIR FLOW

FIGS. 5.36 THROUGH 5.38. THE FOLIAGE OF THE TREES BLOCKS THE AIR FLOW AT THAT LEVEL. AIR SPEED IS INCREASED AT THE TRUNK LEVEL WHICH FORCES THE AIR FLOW UPWARD AND THEN IS REVERSED THROUGH THE BUILDING. AIR FLOW IS NORMAL THROUGH THE OTHER BUILDING SECTIONS.

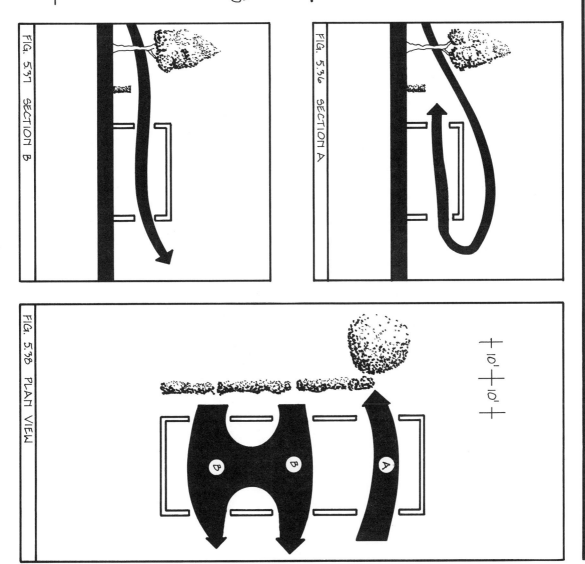

FIG. 5.36 SECTION A

FIG. 5.37 SECTION B

FIG. 5.38 PLAN VIEW

FIG. 5.39 ILLUSTRATES THE DESIRED DIRECTION OF THE AIR FLOW WITHIN THE LIVING AREA.

FIG. 5.40 SHOWS THE INTERNAL AIR MOTION CREATED WHEN THE HOT AIR SUPPLY IS LOCATED AWAY FROM THE WINDOW. THIS CONDITION CAN BE CORRECTED BY LOCATING THE AIR SUPPLY UNDER THE WINDOW. THE NEW AIR MOTION IS SHOWN IN FIG. 5.41. 24

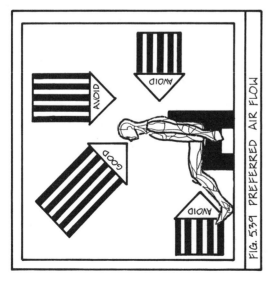

FIG. 5.39 PREFERRED AIR FLOW

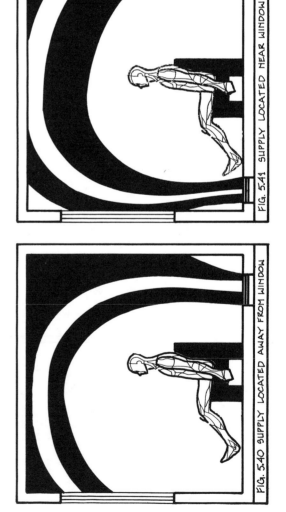

FIG. 5.41 SUPPLY LOCATED NEAR WINDOW

FIG. 5.40 SUPPLY LOCATED AWAY FROM WINDOW

FIGS. 5.42 AND 5.43 SHOW
THE VARIOUS INTERIOR AIR
MOTIONS CREATED BY LO-
CATING THE HOT AIR SUPPLY
IN DIFFERENT POSITIONS.

FIGS. 5.44 AND 5.45
ILLUSTRATE THE INTERIOR
AIR MOTIONS OF COLD AIR
SUPPLIED THROUGH THE
SAME LOCATIONS.

FROM THESE DRAWINGS
IT CAN BE SEEN THAT HOT
AND COLD AIR SHOULD NOT
BE SUPPLIED THROUGH
THE SAME LOCATION. 25

STAGNANT AIR

FIG. 5.42 WARM AIR SUPPLIED THROUGH THE WALL

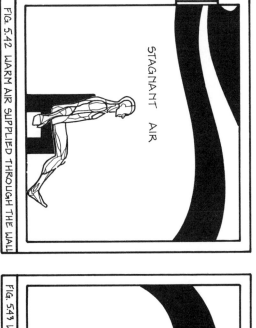

FIG. 5.43 WARM AIR SUPPLIED THROUGH THE FLOOR

FIG. 5.44 COOL AIR SUPPLIED THROUGH THE WALL

STAGNANT AIR

FIG. 5.46 COOL AIR SUPPLIED THROUGH THE FLOOR

TEMPERATURE STRATIFICATION

FIG. 5.46 ILLUSTRATES THE VARIOUS TEMPERATURE LAYERS THAT ARE FORMED WITHIN A ROOM. IT CAN BE SEEN THAT THE LOWER AREA IS CHARACTERIZED BY LOWER TEMPERATURES; YET IT IS IN THIS AREA THAT THE INHABITANTS SPEND OVER 80% OF THEIR TIME.

TEMPERATURE STRATIFICATION SHOULD BE CONSIDERED WHEN INSTALLING THE THERMOSTAT.

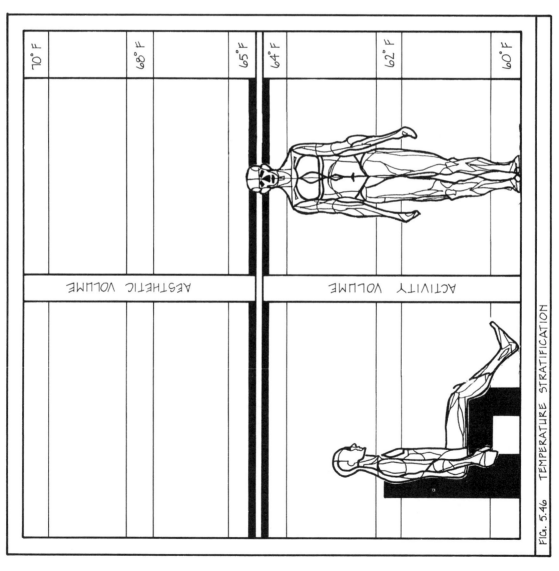

70° F

68° F

65° F

64° F

62° F

60° F

AESTHETIC VOLUME

ACTIVITY VOLUME

FIG. 5.46   TEMPERATURE STRATIFICATION

AIR FLOW IN ATTICS

PROPERLY DESIGNED
AND VENTILATED ATTICS
CAN REDUCE HEAT GAINS
BY AS MUCH AS 25%.

FIG. 5.47 SHOWS A
PROPERLY DESIGNED
GABLE ROOF AND ITS AIR
FLOW PATTERN.

FIG. 5.48 SHOWS A TYP-
ICAL FLAT ROOF ATTIC AND
ITS AIR FLOW PATTERN.

FIG. 5.49 ILLUSTRATES
THE SAME FLAT ROOF BUT
WITH ANGLED SCREENS.
THESE REDUCE AIR STAG-
NATION AND HEAT BUILD-UP.

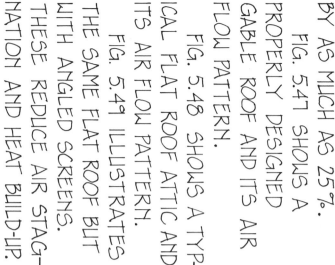

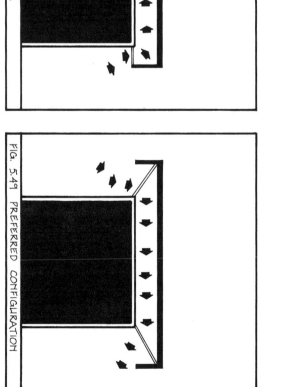

FIG. 5.48 STAGNANT AIR

FIG. 5.49 PREFERRED CONFIGURATION

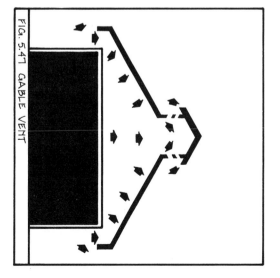

FIG. 5.47 GABLE VENT

THE MAIN GOAL OF ENERGY CONSCIOUS DESIGN IS TO
ACHIEVE A MAJOR REDUCTION IN THE OVERALL ENERGY
CONSUMPTION THROUGH PROPER BUILDING DESIGN AND
CONSTRUCTION.

THIS SECTION STUDIES THE VARIOUS BUILDING COMPO-
NENTS IN TERMS OF THEIR THERMAL CHARACTERISTICS
AND HOW THESE ARE AFFECTED BY THE VARIOUS CLI-
MATIC FACTORS.

IT IS ESTIMATED THAT THROUGH THE CORRECT USE
OF INSULATION, THE AVERAGE HOME CAN REDUCE ITS
ENERGY CONSUMPTION BY OVER 40%.   THEREFORE,
EMPHASIS MUST BE PLACED ON THE PROPER INSULATION
OF EACH COMPONENT. THE USER CAN APPLY THE
INFORMATION GIVEN IN THIS SECTION TO NEW CONSTRUC-
TION AS WELL AS TO RETROFITTING EXISTING PROJECTS.

IT IS GENERALLY ASSUM-
ED THAT HEAT LOSS IS THE
ONLY THERMAL TRAIT OF
FOUNDATIONS, SINCE GROUND
TEMPERATURES ARE EQUAL
TO OR LESS THAN ROOM TEM-
PERATURES DURING THE SUM-
MER MONTHS.

WHEN DESIGNING FOUNDA-
TIONS, PRECISE KNOWLEDGE
OF FROST PENETRATION
SHOULD BE OBTAINED. IN-
SULATION SHOULD BE
PLACED BEYOND THIS
DEPTH.

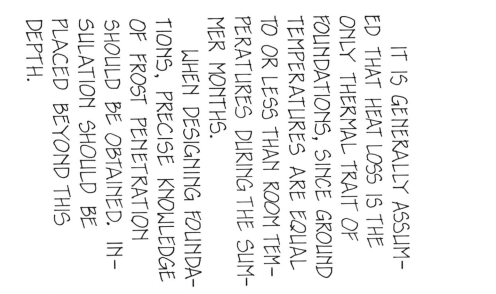

FIG. 6.2 ANGLED INSULATION

INSULATION

FROST LINE

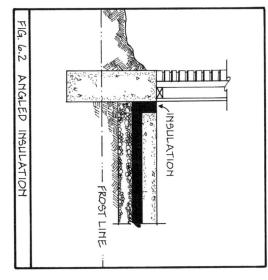

FIG. 6.1 VERTICAL INSULATION

VAPOR BARRIER AND INSULATION

INSULATION

FROST LINE

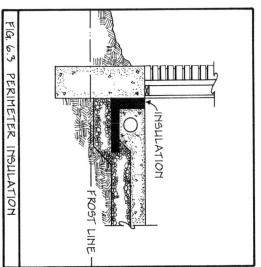

FIG. 6.3 PERIMETER INSULATION

INSULATION

FROST LINE

FIGS. 6.4 THROUGH 6.6 ILLUSTRATE VARIOUS FOUNDATION TYPES AND THE PROPER WAY TO INSULATE THEM. 26

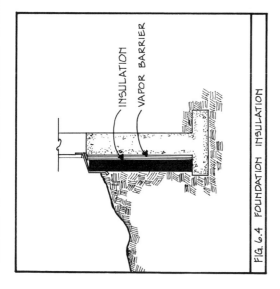

INSULATION
VAPOR BARRIER

FIG. 6.4 FOUNDATION INSULATION

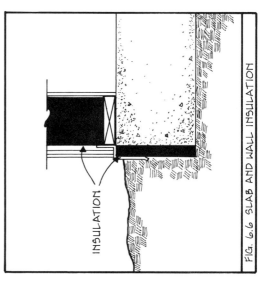

INSULATION

FIG. 6.6 SLAB AND WALL INSULATION

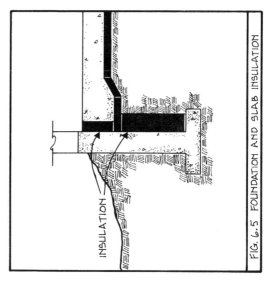

INSULATION

FIG. 6.5 FOUNDATION AND SLAB INSULATION

FOUNDATIONS AND SLABS

FIGS. 6.7 AND 6.8 ILLUS-
TRATE ADDITIONAL INSULAT-
ED FOUNDATIONS. FIG. 6.9
SHOWS A COMPLETELY IN-
SULATED FOUNDATION AND
FLOOR SLAB. NOTE: THE
INSULATION CAN BE FIBER-
GLASS, CORK OR NEO-
PRENE.

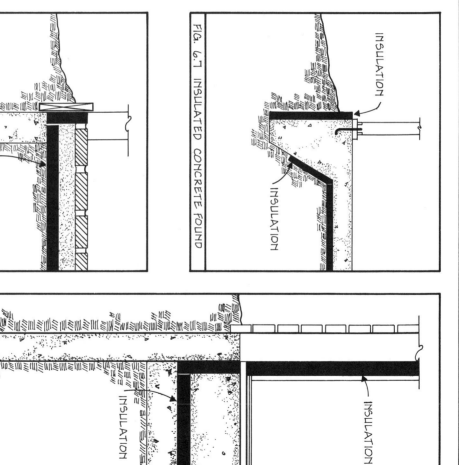

FIG. 6.8 INSULATED BRICK SLAB

INSULATION

FIG. 6.7 INSULATED CONCRETE FOUND

INSULATION

INSULATION

FIG. 6.9 INSULATED FLOATED SLAB

INSULATION

INSULATION

IN BUILDINGS WITH TWO
OR MORE LEVELS, THE CEIL-
ING CAN BE DESIGNED AS AN
INTEGRAL PART OF THE FLOOR.
FIGS. 6.10 AND 6.11 DE-
PICT THE WOOD JOIST FLOOR
CEILING SYSTEM. NOTE THE
POSSIBILITY OF INSTALLING
INSULATION BETWEEN THE
JOISTS AND COVERING IT
WITH MORE PLANKING OR
SHEET ROCK. THE USE OF
INSULATION IN THE BUILDING'S
INTERIOR INTRODUCES THE DE-
SIGN CONCEPT OF CONSTRUCT-
ING BUILDINGS AS A SERIES
OF INDIVIDUALLY INSULATED
ROOMS WITH SEPARATE
ENVIRONMENTAL CONTROLS.

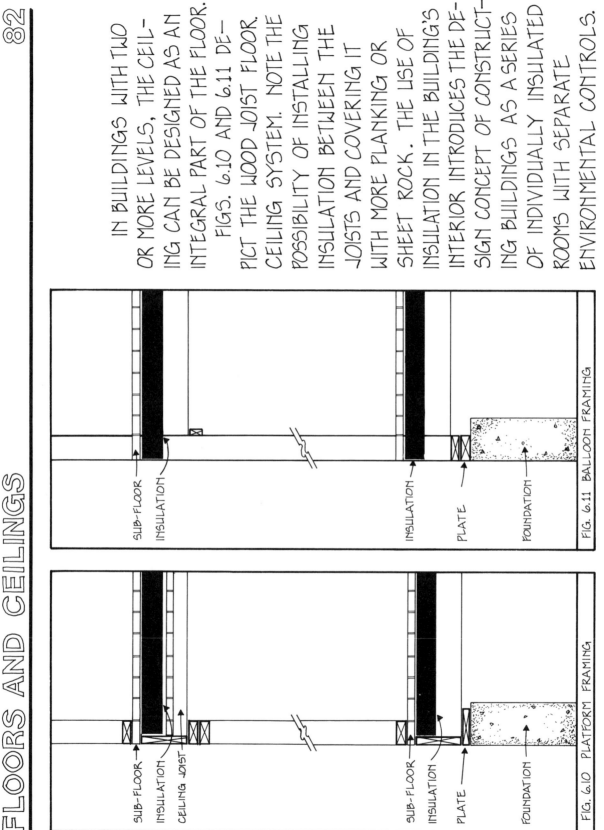

FIG. 6.10 PLATFORM FRAMING

SUB-FLOOR
INSULATION
CEILING JOIST

SUB-FLOOR
INSULATION
PLATE

FOUNDATION

FIG. 6.11 BALLOON FRAMING

SUB-FLOOR
INSULATION

INSULATION
PLATE

FOUNDATION

PLANK AND BEAM CONSTRUCTION USES LARGER WOOD BEAMS THAN DOES JOIST CONSTRUCTION, BUT IN THE FORMER, THE MEMBERS ARE PLACED FARTHER APART. PLANK FLOOR SYSTEMS PROVIDE A MINIMUM FINISH GRADE TO FLOOR SEPARATION. DUE TO THE INCREASED DEPTH OF THE BEAMS, IT IS POSSIBLE TO INSULATE THE FLOORS AND MAINTAIN THE EXPOSED BEAM SYSTEM AS AN ARCHITECTURAL ELEMENT. FIG. 6.12.

STEEL AND CONCRETE SYSTEMS OFFER LARGER SPANS THAN DO TIMBER SYSTEMS, INCREASED FIRE RE-SISTANCE AND GREATER STABILITY. THERE ARE SEV-ERAL WAYS TO INSULATE SUCH SYSTEMS. SPRAY IN-SULATION IS OFTEN USED; HOWEVER, HANGING THE CORRECT THICKNESS OF BATT AND OTHER TYPES OF INSULATION WILL YIELD THE SAME RESULTS.

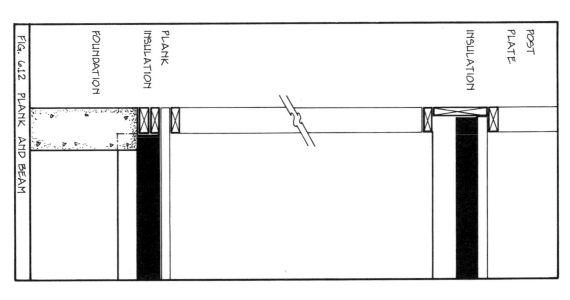

POST
PLATE
INSULATION

PLANK
INSULATION

FOUNDATION

FIG. 6.12 PLANK AND BEAM

AN EXCELLENT ENERGY
SAVING MEASURE IS TO USE
2×6 FRAMING MEMBERS
INSTEAD OF THE TRADITION-
AL 2×4 MEMBERS. THE LAR-
GER MEMBERS ARE SPACED
24" O.C. THE ADDED DEPTH
ALLOWS FOR INCREASED
THICKNESS IN INSULATION.
THE AMOUNT OF WOOD
USED IS ABOUT THE SAME
BUT THERE ARE LABOR
SAVINGS SINCE 2×6'S ARE
EASIER TO FRAME. FIG. 6.15.

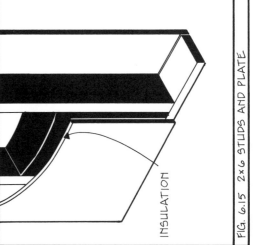

INSULATION

FIG. 6.15 2×6 STUDS AND PLATE.

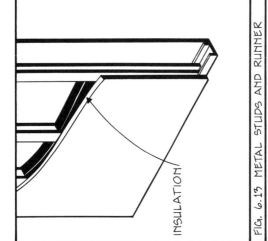

INSULATION

FIG. 6.13 METAL STUDS AND RUNNER

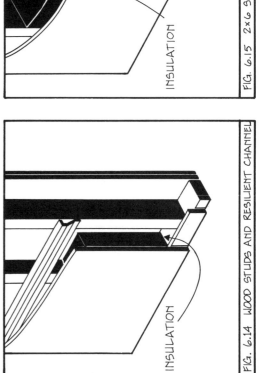

INSULATION

FIG. 6.14 WOOD STUDS AND RESILIENT CHANNEL

MASONRY WALLS ARE USUALLY LEFT EXPOSED, BUT THEY MAY BE FINISHED IN THE INTERIOR. ONE OF SEVERAL WAYS TO INSULATE MASONRY WALLS IS TO FUR THE INTERIOR WITH 2×3'S, 16" O.C.; PLACE BATT INSULATION BETWEEN THE STUDS, AND COVER THE OPENING WITH THE DESIRED FINISH. FIG. 6.16.

A COMMON PRACTICE IS TO BLOW INSULATION DOWN THE WALL CAVITY. THIS PROCEDURE, HOWEVER, OFFERS SOME DRAWBACKS. WITH TIME AND MOISTURE, THE INSULATION SHRINKS DOWN TOWARDS THE BOTTOM OF THE WALL, LEAVING THE TOP COMPLETELY UNINSULATED.

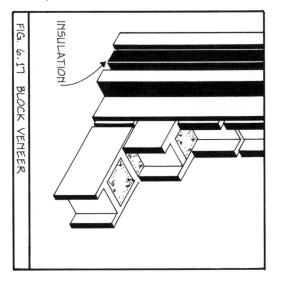

FIG. 6.17 BLOCK VENEER

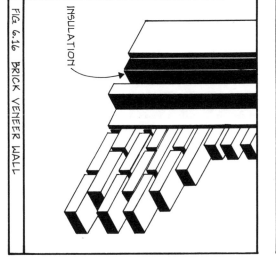

FIG. 6.16 BRICK VENEER WALL

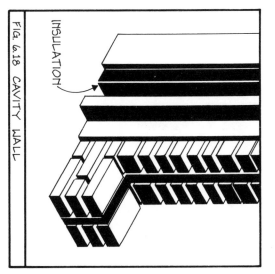

FIG. 6.18 CAVITY WALL

FIGS. 6.19 THROUGH 6.21 SHOW OTHER TYPES OF MASONRY WALLS AND HOW TO INSULATE THEM.

IT IS POSSIBLE TO FILL-IN THE WALL CAVITIES WITH ALUMINUM OXIDE PELLETS, STEEL WOOL OR PEBBLES TO INCREASE THE THERMAL CAPACITY OF THE WALL.

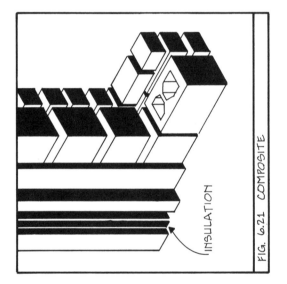

INSULATION

FIG. 6.21 COMPOSITE

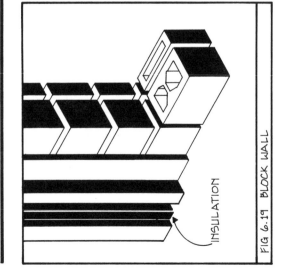

INSULATION

FIG 6.19 BLOCK WALL

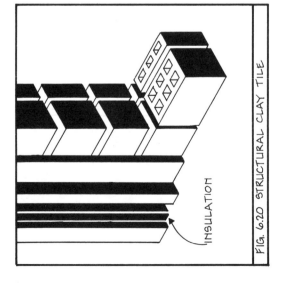

INSULATION

FIG. 6.20 STRUCTURAL CLAY TILE

FIG. 6.22 SHOWS A HOL-
LOW PLASTER PARTITION
WITH CHANNEL STUDS.

FIG. 6.23 SHOWS THE
SAME TYPE OF WALL WITH
TRUSSED STUDS.

FIG. 6.24 SHOWS THE
WALL WITH BRACED DOUBLE
STUDS. THIS WALL CAN
ACCOMMODATE MECHANICAL
EQUIPMENT WITHIN IT'S
CAVITY SPACE. IT ALSO
ALLOWS FOR THE INSTAL-
LATION OF THICKER INSU-
LATION.

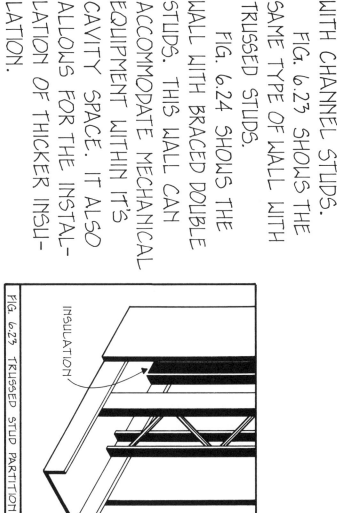

INSULATION

FIG. 6.23 TRUSSED STUD PARTITION

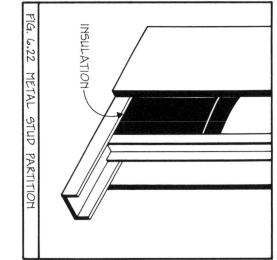

INSULATION

FIG. 6.22 METAL STUD PARTITION

INSULATION

FIG. 6.24 DOUBLE STUD PARTITION

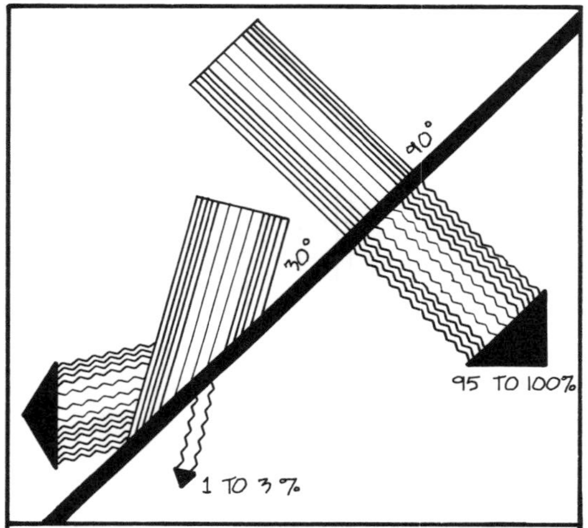

HEAT GAINS OR LOSSES CAN BE CONTROLLED THROUGH PROPER USE OF THE WINDOW'S INSULATIVE, REFLECTIVE, ABSORBENT AND SHADING CHARACTERISTICS.

THERMAL EXPANSION SHOULD BE STUDIED WHEN USING TINTED OR REFLECTIVE COATED GLASSES SINCE THESE ABSORB HIGHER HEAT PERCENTAGES.

AS A RULE, GLASS PERMITS SUN RADIATION OF WAVELENGTHS 0.4 TO 2.5 MICRONS TO PASS THROUGH IT. AS THIS RADIANT ENERGY COLLIDES WITH OPAQUE OBJECTS ON THE OTHER SIDE OF THE GLASS, IT'S WAVELENGTH INCREASES TO 11 MICRONS. GLASS ACTS AS AN OPAQUE BARRIER TO LIGHT OF THIS WAVELENGTH THEREBY TRAPPING THE SUN'S ENERGY. FIG. 6.25 ILLUSTRATES HOW THE AMOUNT OF LIGHT PENETRATING A PIECE OF GLASS IS DEPENDENT ON THE ANGLE OF INCIDENCE. THE OPTIMUM ANGLE OF INCIDENCE IS 90°. WHEN SUNLIGHT STRIKES THE GLASS AT 30° OR LESS, THE MOST RADIATION IS REFLECTED.

40°

90°

95 TO 100%

1 TO 3 %

FIG. 6.25 LIGHT PENETRATION

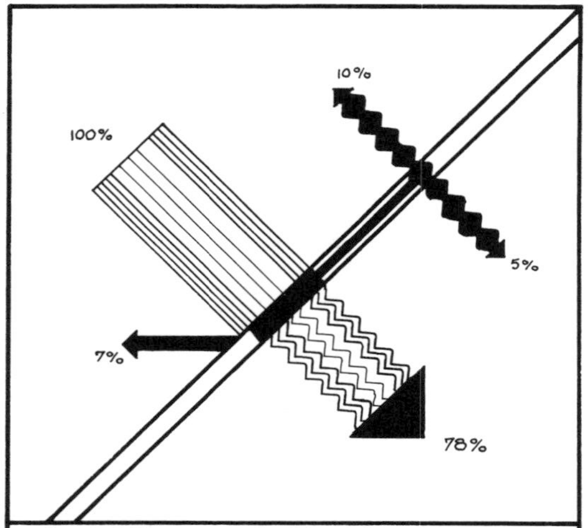

10%

5%

78%

100%

7%

FIG. 6.25 A. LIGHT PENETRATION

FIGS. 6.26 AND 6.27 SHOW THE ENERGY FLOW THAT TAKES PLACE WHEN WINDOWS RUN FROM FLOOR TO CEILING IN BOTH THE COOLING AND HEATING CYCLES.

FIGS. 6.28 AND 6.29 ILLUSTRATE HOW ENERGY CAN BE SAVED THROUGH PROPER WINDOW DESIGN.

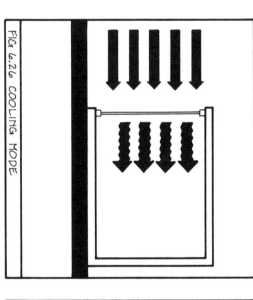

FIG. 6.26 COOLING MODE

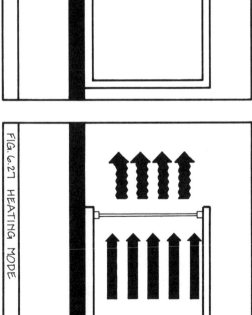

FIG. 6.27 HEATING MODE

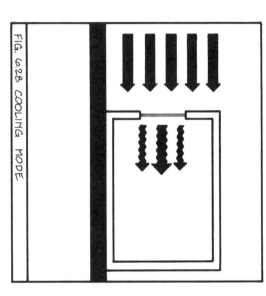

FIG. 6.28 COOLING MODE

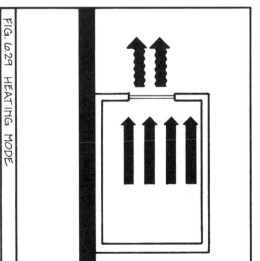

FIG. 6.29 HEATING MODE

IN ADDITION TO DECORATIVE FUNCTIONS, CURTAINS CAN BE USED TO REDUCE THE HEAT LOSSES THAT OCCUR DURING THE COLD MONTHS AS WELL AS THE HEAT GAINS DURING THE WARMER MONTHS.

FIG. 6.30 ILLUSTRATES HOW AIR MOVES DOWN AND ACROSS THE COLD GLASS AND FLOWS ONTO THE FLOOR AND LIVING LEVELS.

FIG. 6.31 SHOWS HOW THIS CONDITION CAN BE COR-RECTED. THE PLYWOOD BOX OVER THE CURTAIN TOP PREVENTS WARM CEILING AIR FROM MOVING BETWEEN THE GLASS AND CURTAIN. THE CURTAIN SHOULD DROP AT LEAST 12" BELOW THE WINDOW SILL FOR IT TO BE EFFECTIVE. THE OPTIMUM CONDITION WOULD BE FOR IT TO DROP TO THE FLOOR.[27]

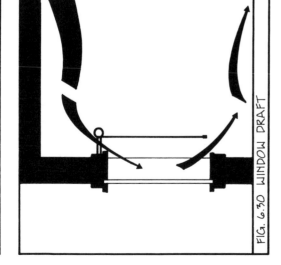

FIG. 6.30 WINDOW DRAFT

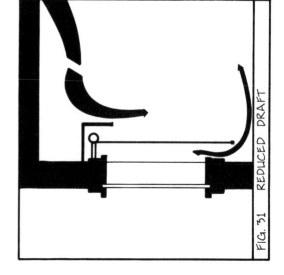

FIG. 31 REDUCED DRAFT

PLASTIC STORM WINDOWS HAVE A LIMITED LIFE SPAN BUT THEIR ENERGY SAVING EFFICIENCY IS HIGH. THEIR COST IS MINIMUM AND THEIR INSTALLATION IS AS SIMPLE AS PUSHING THUMB TACKS. AVOID USING PLASTICS OF LESS THAN 4 MIL THICKNESS; 6 MIL IS RECOMMENDED. TO INSTALL, CUT A SHEET LARGER THAN THE WINDOW, AND ROLL ENDS AS SHOWN IN FIG. 6.32. TACK OR STAPLE EDGES INTO THE WINDOW FRAME. USE DUCT TAPE IF THE WINDOW HAS A METAL FRAME.

IT IS ALSO POSSIBLE TO BUILD A MOUNTING FRAME WHICH CAN BE REMOVED WHEN NOT NEEDED. SEE FIG. 6.33. PLASTIC STORM WINDOWS ARE NOT CLEAR; THEY ARE TRANSLUCENT. LIGHT WILL COME THROUGH, BUT THE USER WILL NOT BE ABLE TO SEE CLEARLY THROUGH THEM. [28]

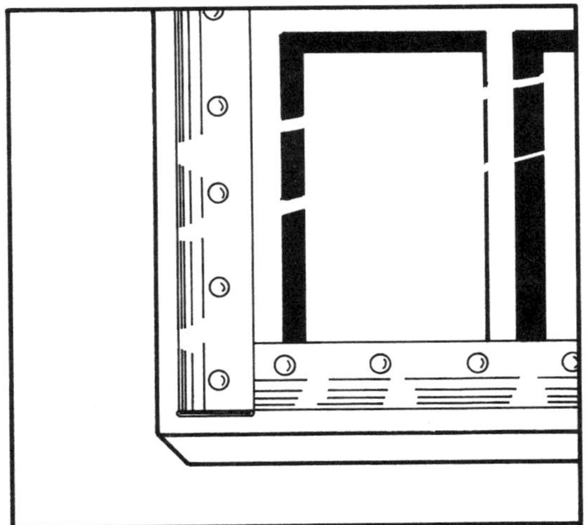

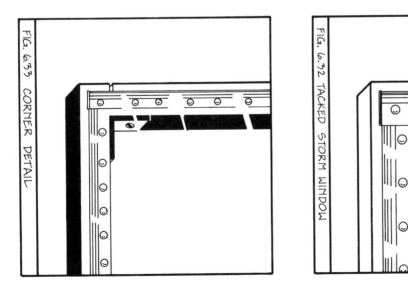

FIG. 6.32 TACKED STORM WINDOW

FIG. 6.33 CORNER DETAIL

FIG. 6.34 SHOWS A FLAT CANTILEVERED OVERHANG. THIS TYPE OF CONSTRUCTION CAUSES HEAT TO ACCUMULATE UNDER THE FLAP. THIS INCREASES UNDESIRABLE HEAT GAINS.

FIG. 6.35 SOLVES THE HEAT ACCUMULATION PROBLEM BY USING A LOUVERED OVERHANG.

FIG. 6.35 ILLUSTRATES A SLOPED OVERHANG WITH A FOLDING FLAP. BY SEPARATING THE OVERHANG FROM THE BUILDING, THERE IS NO HEAT ACCUMULATION. THE FOLDING FLAP ALLOWS SUNLIGHT TO REACH THE INTERIOR AT THE USER'S DISCRETION.

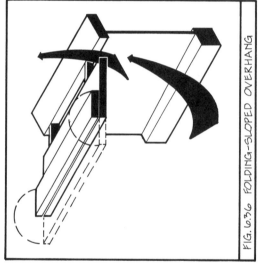

FIG. 6.36 FOLDING-SLOPED OVERHANG

HEAT ACCUMULATION

FIG. 6.34 FLAT OVERHANG

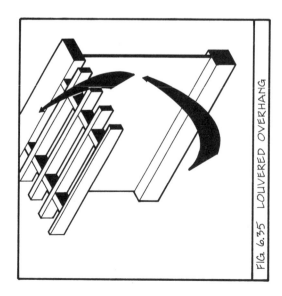

FIG. 6.35 LOUVERED OVERHANG

FIG. 6.37 SHOWS THE TYPE OF SCREENS USED FOR SOUTHERN EXPOSURES. IN THE CASE WHERE THE PREVAILING VIEW IS TO THE SOUTH, THE DESIGNER SHOULD USE A LOUVER OF 2" TO 3" IN WIDTH AND REDUCE THE SPACING BETWEEN THEM. THIS WILL YIELD A HIGHER VIEW PENETRATION WITH NO INCREASE IN RADIATION INFILTRATION.

FIG. 6.38 SHOWS A VERTICAL SCREEN. THESE SHOULD BE USED FOR EAST AND WEST EXPOSURES. IN ADDITION TO SIZE AND SHAPE, THE USER SHOULD CONSIDER COLOR WHEN DESIGNING SCREENS SINCE CERTAIN COLORS ARE MORE EFFECTIVE THAN OTHERS WHEN REFLECTING HEAT. FOR EXAMPLE, THE PERCENTAGE OF THE TOTAL INCIDENT HEAT REFLECTED BY LIGHT GRAY PAINT IS 25, BY LIGHT GREEN 50, BY WHITE 75 AND BY ALUMINUM FOIL 95.

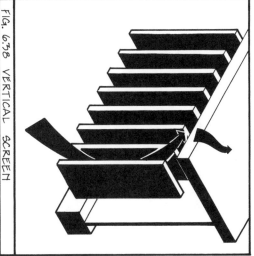

FIG. 6.38 VERTICAL SCREEN

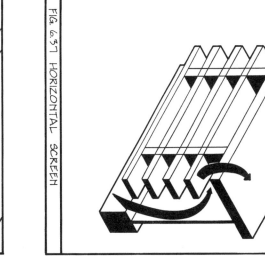

FIG. 6.37 HORIZONTAL SCREEN

EXTERIOR DOORS SHOULD MAKE A TIGHT SEAL WHEN CLOSED AND SHOULD BE INSULATED TO REDUCE HEAT GAIN AND LOSS. HOWEVER, EVEN WITH THESE ENERGY SAVING PROCEDURES, EXTERIOR DOORS AND ENTRIES REMAIN ENERGY WASTEFUL. THE BEST WAY TO EFFECTIVELY REDUCE THIS WASTE IS TO DESIGN ENTRY FOYERS. FIGS. 6.39 AND 6.40 ILLUSTRATE TWO FOYER DESIGNS. IT IS ESSENTIAL THAT THE OVERALL LENGTH "L", BE NO LESS THAN 5'-0", OTHERWISE, THE PERSON ENTERING OR LEAVING WOULD BE FORCED TO OPEN THE SECOND DOOR BEFORE THE FIRST ONE COULD BE CLOSED.

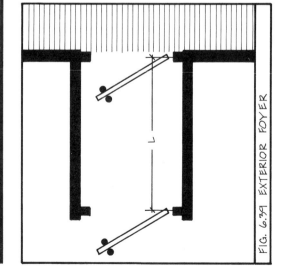

FIG. 6.39 EXTERIOR FOYER.

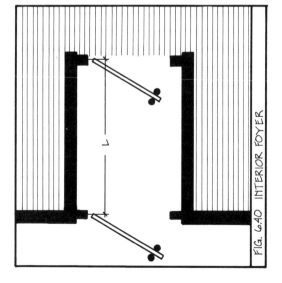

FIG. 6.40 INTERIOR FOYER.

COMPRESSION WEATHER STRIPPING, WHEN PROPERLY APPLIED, PRODUCES A COMPLETELY WEATHERTIGHT SEAL. ALL CAULKING SHOULD BE APPLIED OVER CLEAN, DRY AND SOLID SURFACES. CRACKS OF 3/16" OR MORE SHOULD BE FILLED WITHIN 1/4" OF THE SURFACE WITH BACKUP MATERIAL.[29] FIGS. 6.41 AND 6.42 SHOW SOME DO'S AND DONT'S.

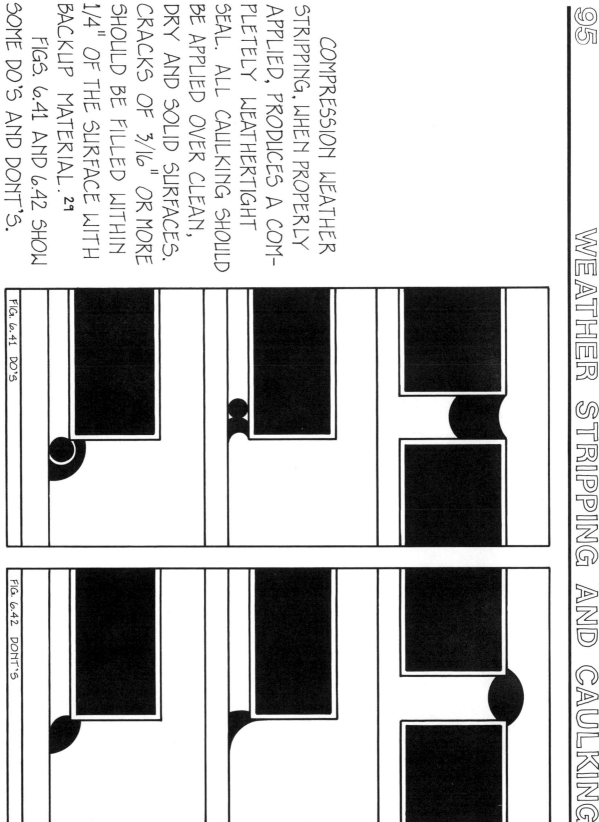

FIG. 6.41 DO'S

FIG. 6.42 DONT'S

FIREPLACES CAN PRO-
VIDE A GREAT DEAL OF
HEAT AND COMFORT WHEN
PROPERLY DESIGNED. THE
BEST FIREPLACE IS SHALLOW
AND HIGH. FIGS. 6.43 AND
6.44 SHOW THE CORRECT
PROPORTIONS FOR THE
FIREPLACE. 30

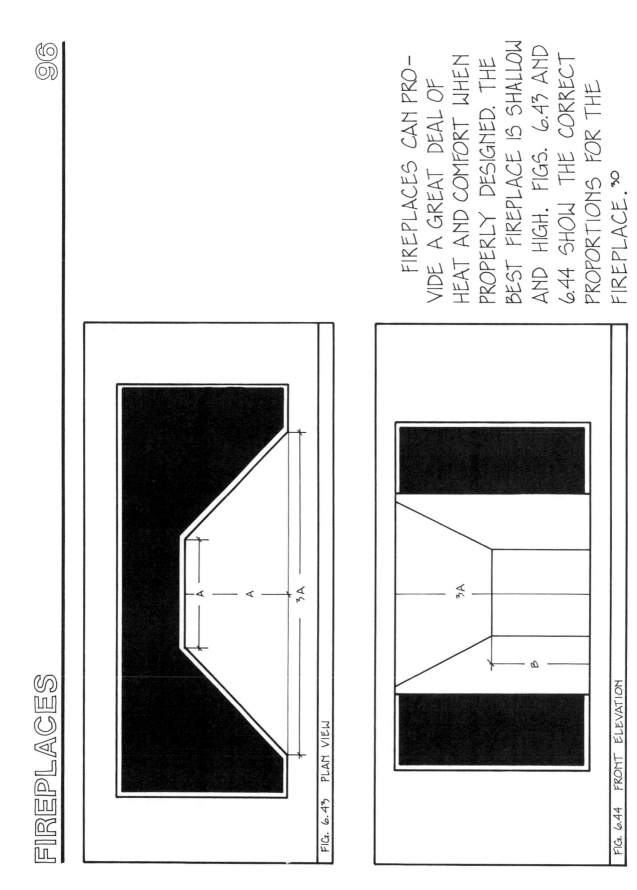

FIG. 6.43 PLAN VIEW

FIG. 6.44 FRONT ELEVATION

THE LOCATION OF THE FIREPLACE IS AN ASPECT OFTEN NEGLECTED BUT ONE WHICH IS CRUCIAL TO THE CONSERVATION OF THE ENERGY IT PRODUCES. WHENEVER POSSIBLE THE FIREPLACE SHOULD BE CENTRALLY LOCATED.

THE SLOPED BACK WALL "B", SHOULD BEGIN ITS INCLINE ABOUT 15" ABOVE THE HEARTH AND SHOULD MEET THE FRONT OF THE SMOKE SHELF.

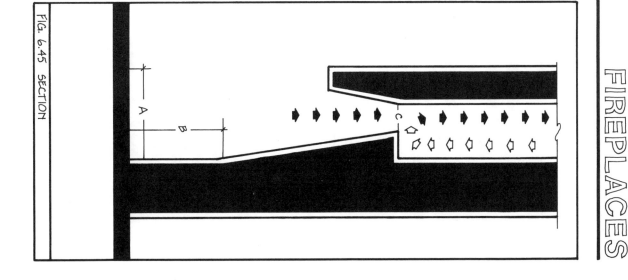

FIG. 6.45 SECTION

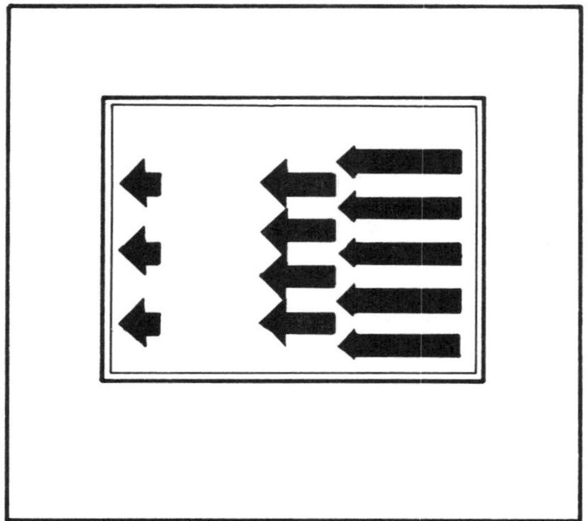

HEAT MAY BE LOST IN
THREE WAYS: CONDUC-
TION, CONVECTION, AND
RADIATION.

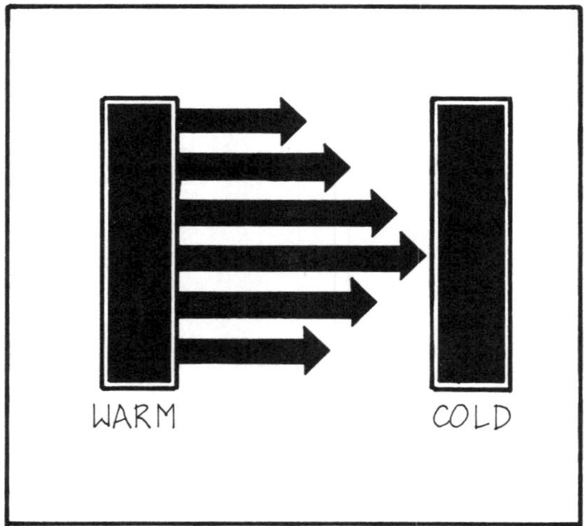

CONDUCTION IS THE
HEAT TRANSFER FROM
WARM TO COOLER AREAS
WITHIN THE SAME MATERIAL.
CONVECTION IS HEAT
TRANSFER IN AIR FROM
WARM TO COOLER AREAS.
RADIATION IS HEAT
TRANSFER FROM WARM
TO COOLER AREAS
THROUGH ELECTROMAG-
NETIC WAVES.

FIG. 6.46 CONDUCTION

FIG. 6.47 CONVECTION

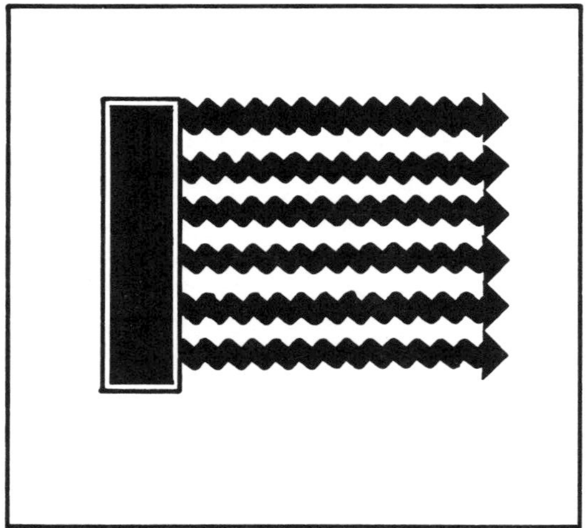

WARM

COLD

FIG. 6.48 RADIATION

FIG. 6.49 SHOWS THE HEAT FLOW FROM THE IN-
TERIOR TO THE EXTERIOR SPACE THROUGH A WALL SEC-
TION. AS HEAT MOVES FROM ONE MATERIAL TO AN-
OTHER, ITS TEMPERATURE DROPS. EACH MATERIAL IN
THE WALL HAS A RESISTANCE VALUE "R". THE TOTAL
RESISTANCE "R" OF THE WALL IS THE SUM OF THE IN-
DIVIDUAL COMPONENT RESISTANCES. THE RECIPRO-
CAL OF R, 1/R, IS CALLED THE "U" VALUE AND IT
IS USED TO CALCULATE HOW MUCH HEAT IS LOST
IN BTU'S THROUGH ONE SQUARE FOOT OF
MATERIAL.

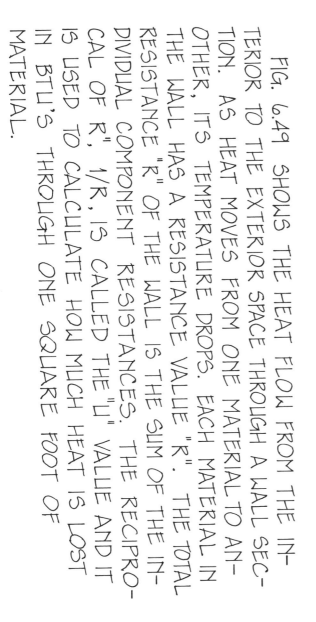

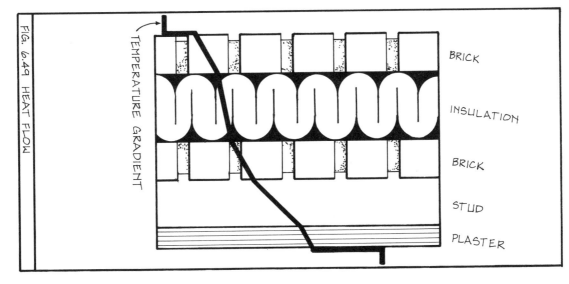

FIG. 6.49 HEAT FLOW

TEMPERATURE GRADIENT

BRICK

INSULATION

BRICK

STUD

PLASTER

$$Q = A [U(t_i - t_o)]$$

WHERE Q = HEAT LOSS IN BTU'S PER HOUR
   A = AREA OF THE ASSEMBLY IN SQUARE FEET
   U = U VALUE OF THE ASSEMBLY
   t_i = INDOOR TEMPERATURE
   t_o = OUT DOOR TEMPERATURE

ONCE THE U VALUES HAVE BEEN DETERMINED FOR ALL BUILDING SECTIONS, THEY ARE PLUGGED INTO THE FORMULA.

IT IS DETERMINED BY THE DESIGNER IN ACCORD-ANCE WITH DAILY AND SEASONAL STANDARDS. IN ADDITION TO THIS, IT IS NECESSARY TO COMPUTE THE AMOUNT OF HEAT LOSS THAT TAKES PLACE THROUGH WINDOWS AND DOORS. THE SUMMATION OF ALL THE VALUES OBTAINED WILL YIELD THE AMOUNT OF HEAT THAT IS LOST IN THE BUILDING FOR ONE HOUR. THIS IS EQUIVALENT TO THE HEAT LOAD DEMAND FOR THE MECHANICAL SYSTEM.

NEXT WE CALCULATE THE ANNUAL ENERGY USED FOR HEATING. THIS IS DONE WITH THE FORMULA:

$$X = \frac{H(t - t_q)}{(t_i - t_o)}$$

WHERE X = AVERAGE HEATING REQUIREMENT FOR HEATING SEASON/HOUR
H = HEAT LOSS CALCULATED FOR THE DESIGN CONDITIONS
t = AVERAGE INDOOR TEMPERATURE FOR THE SEASON
t_q = AVERAGE OUTDOOR TEMPERATURE FOR THE SEASON
t_i = INDOOR DESIGN TEMPERATURE
t_o = OUTDOOR DESIGN TEMPERATURE

THE VALUE OBTAINED FOR X IS AN AVERAGE PER HOUR FOR THE HEATING SEASON. THEREFORE, IT MUST BE MULTIPLIED BY THE TOTAL NUMBER OF HOURS IN THE SEASON, TO OBTAIN THE TOTAL ANNUAL CONSUMPTION OF ENERGY FOR HEATING. FOR EXAMPLE, THERE ARE 212 DAYS FROM OCT. 1st. TO MAY 1st.; SO 212 × 24 = 5,088. THE TOTAL ANNUAL CONSUMPTION OF ENERGY FOR HEATING WILL BE (5,088)X. THIS FIGURE SHOULD BE COMPARED WITH THE TOTAL ANNUAL RADIATION RECEIVED IN AN AREA TO DETERMINE THE PER-CENTAGE OF THE LOAD THAT THE SUN WILL BE ABLE TO SUPPLY.

THE PURPOSE OF THIS LIST IS TO INTRODUCE
DESIGN GUIDELINES. IT SHOULD BE NOTED, HOWEVER,
THAT THESE RULES ARE GENERIC IN NATURE;
THEREFORE SPECIFIC SITE AND BUILDING CONDI-
TIONS MAY NEGATE THE VALIDITY OF THEIR IM-
PLEMENTATION. THE DESIGNER SHOULD USE THE
LIST TO ESTABLISH A POINT OF REFERENCE FROM
WHICH THE DESIGN MAY EVOLVE.

BUILDING CONFIG. & ORIENT. / SITE ORIENTATION		COOL	TEMPERATE	HOT-HUMID	HOT-ARID
FLAT SITE	SUN	SOUTHEAST	SOUTH TO SOUTHEAST	SOUTH	SOUTH
FLAT SITE	WIND	SHELTERED FROM NORTH AND WEST WINDS. AVOID EXPOSURE TO WINTER WINDS. EXPOSE TO SUMMER WINDS.	SHELTERED FROM NORTH-WEST. OPEN TO PREVAILING SUMMER BREEZES.	EXPOSE TO PREVAILING WINDS.	
SLOPED SITE	PRECIPITATION	NEAR LARGE BODY OF WATER ALLOW BUILD-UP OF SNOW	CLOSE TO WATER BUT AVOID COASTAL FOG. ALLOW BUILD-UP OF SNOW	NEAR ANY WATER	NEAR ANY WATER
SLOPED SITE	SUN	SOUTH TO SOUTHEAST	SOUTH TO SOUTHEAST	SOUTH	EAST TO SOUTHEAST
SLOPED SITE	WIND	LOW POSITION FOR WIND SHELTER	LOW POSITION FOR WIND SHELTER	HIGH POSITION TO CATCH WIND	LOW POSITION FOR COLD AIR FLOW
CUBE	SUN	ORIENT NW-SE 30 ALL SIDES RECEIVE SUN	ORIENT NW-SE 30 ALL SIDES RECEIVE SUN	ORIENT E-W TO FREE A FACADE FROM RECEIVING DIRECT SUN	ORIENT E-W TO FREE A FACADE FROM RECEIVING DIRECT SUN
CUBE	WIND	ORIENT POINT OF CUBE TOWARD PREVAILING WINDS TO DEFLECT THE WIND AND PROTECT THE FRONT OF THE BUILDING.	ORIENT POINT OF CUBE TOWARD PREVAILING WINDS TO DEFLECT THE WIND AND PROTECT THE FRONT OF THE BUILDING.	ORIENT FLAT SURFACE PERPENDICULAR TO PREVAILING WIND FOR COOLING	ORIENT FLAT SURFACE PERPENDICULAR TO PREVAILING WIND FOR COOLING

SITE DEVELOPMENT AND BUILDING INTEGRATION 104

			COOL	TEMPERATE	HOT-HUMID	HOT-ARID
BUILDING CONFIGURATION & ORIENTATION	ATRIUM	SUN		ORIENT NW-SE SO ALL SIDES RECEIVE SUN	ORIENT E-W TO FREE A FACADE FROM RECEIVING DIRECT SUN	ORIENT E-W TO FREE A FACADE FROM RECEIVING DIRECT SUN
		WIND		ORIENT POINT OF CUBE TOWARD PREVAILING WINDS TO DEFLECT THE WIND AND PROTECT THE FRONT OF THE BUILDING	ORIENT FLAT SURFACE PERPENDICULAR TO PREVAILING WIND FOR COOLING	ORIENT FLAT SURFACE PERPENDICULAR TO PREVAILING WIND FOR COOLING
	CHANNEL	SUN			ORIENT SO AS NOT TO FORM A HEAT TRAP.	ORIENT SO AS NOT TO FORM A HEAT TRAP.
		WIND			ORIENT OPEN SIDE OF CHANNEL TOWARD PREVAILING WINDS.	ORIENT OPEN SIDE OF CHANNEL TOWARD PREVAILING WINDS.
	"L" SHAPE	SUN	ORIENT TO CREATE A HEAT TRAP.	ORIENT TO CREATE A HEAT TRAP.	ORIENT SO AS NOT TO FORM A HEAT TRAP.	ORIENT SO AS NOT TO FORM A HEAT TRAP.
		WIND	PROTECT INTERIOR COURT FROM PREVAILING WINDS.	PROTECT INTERIOR COURT FROM PREVAILING WINDS.	CAPTURE PREVAILING WINDS WITH INTERIOR COURT FOR COOLING.	CAPTURE PREVAILING WINDS WITH INTERIOR COURT FOR COOLING.

BUILDING CONFIGURATION & ORIENTATION			COOL	TEMPERATE	HOT-HUMID	HOT-ARID
RECTANGLE	SUN		ORIENT E-W SO LONG SIDE IS TOWARD SUN.	ORIENT E-W SO LONG SIDE IS TOWARD SUN.	ORIENT N-S TO E-W TO RECEIVE MAXIMUM MORNING SUN AND MINIMUM NOON AND AFTERNOON SUN.	ORIENT N-S TO E-W TO RECEIVE MAXIMUM MORNING SUN AND MINIMUM NOON AND AFTERNOON SUN.
	WIND		ORIENT POINT OF BUILDING TOWARD PREVAILING WINDS FOR DEFLECTION OF WIND AND PROTECTION OF FRONT OF BUILDING.	ORIENT POINT OF BUILDING TOWARD PREVAILING WINDS FOR DEFLECTION OF WIND AND PROTECTION OF FRONT OF BUILDING.	ORIENT LONG SURFACE PERPENDICULAR TOWARD PREVAILING WIND FOR COOLING.	ORIENT LONG SURFACE PERPENDICULAR TOWARD PREVAILING WIND FOR COOLING.
CYLINDER					THIS FORM REACTS EQUALLY TO ALL ORIENTATIONS.	
DOME					THIS FORM REACTS EQUALLY TO ALL ORIENTATIONS.	
ADJACENT BUILDINGS	SUN		AVOID BLOCKING SUN. PREFERRED TO REFLECT ADDITIONAL SOLAR INSOLATION ON BUILDING.	AVOID BLOCKING SUN.	AVOID REFLECTING ADDITIONAL SOLAR INSOLATION ON BUILDING.	AVOID REFLECTING ADDITIONAL SOLAR INSOLATION ON BUILDING.
	WIND		USE AS A WIND BREAK FROM PREVAILING WINDS.	USE TO BLOCK WINTER WINDS. AVOID BLOCKING SUMMER BREEZES.	USE TO BLOCK WINTER WINDS AND TO CHANNEL SUMMER BREEZES ON BUILDING. AVOID OBSTRUCTING SUMMER WINDS.	AVOID BLOCKING PREVAILING WINDS.

MAN-MADE ELEMENTS			COOL	TEMPERATE	HOT-HUMID	HOT-ARID
PAVED AREAS		SUN	USE TO REFLECT ADDITIONAL SOLAR INSOLATION TO BUILDING AND TO FORM A WARM AIR POCKET.	USE TO REFLECT ADDITIONAL SOLAR INSOLATION TO BUILDING. SHADE THIS AREA IN SUMMER TO AVOID HEAT BUILD-UP.	AVOID EXCESS BUILD-UP OF SOLAR INSOLATION.	AVOID ANY REFLECTION ON BUILDING AND ADDITIONAL HEAT GAIN.
		WIND	PLACE IN DIRECTION OF PREVAILING WINDS TO CARRY ANY HEAT BUILD-UP TO BUILDING.	PLACE IN DIRECTION OF PREVAILING WINDS TO CARRY ANY HEAT BUILD-UP TO BUILDING.	AVOID PAVED AREAS IN PATH OF SUMMER WINDS	AVOID PAVED AREAS IN PATH OF SUMMER WINDS.
		PRECIPITATION	USE FOR SNOW ACCUMULATION AND ADDITIONAL REFLECTION HEAT GAIN.	USE FOR SNOW ACCUMULATION AND ADDITIONAL REFLECTION HEAT GAIN. USE TO IMPROVE DRAINAGE IN SUMMER.	USE TO DRAIN AWAY ANY PRECIPITATION.	USE TO COLLECT RAINWATER FOR COOLING.
FENCES		SUN	USE TO DEFLECT PREVAILING WINDS. AVOID TRAPPING COLD WINDS.	USE TO DEFLECT WINTER WINDS. USE TO CHANNEL SUMMER BREEZES TO THE BUILDING.	USE TO CHANNEL SUMMER BREEZES TO BUILDING.	USE TO CHANNEL SUMMER WINDS TO THE BUILDING. USE TO TRAP ANY COLD BREEZES.
BERMS		SUN	USE TO INSULATE BUILDING FROM COLD TEMPERATURES.	USE TO INSULATE BUILDING FROM COLD TEMPERATURES.		USE TO INSULATE BUILDING FROM HOT TEMPERATURES.
		WIND	USE AS A WIND BREAK FROM PREVAILING WINDS.	USE AS A WIND BREAK IN WINTER AND TO CHANNEL BREEZES TO BUILDING IN SUMMER.	USE TO DIRECT WIND TO BUILDING.	USE TO CHANNEL WIND TO BUILDING.

NATURAL ELEMENTS		COOL	TEMPERATE	HOT-HUMID	HOT-ARID
DECIDUOUS VEGETATION	SUN	AVOID BLOCKING SUN.	TO SOUTH FOR SUMMER SHADE.	TO SOUTH FOR SUMMER SHADE.	TO SOUTH AND WEST FOR MIDDAY AND AFTERNOON SHADE.
	WIND	ALLOW PASSAGE OF SUMMER BREEZES.	CHANNEL SUMMER BREEZES TO BUILDING.	CHANNEL SUMMER BREEZES TO BUILDING.	USE HIGH CANOPY TYPES CHANNEL WINDS TO TO ALLOW COOLING BREEZES TO STRIKE BUILDING.
ROCK FORMATIONS	SUN	PREFERRED FOR SOLAR REFLECTION. PREFERRED NEAR BUILDING TO ACT AS A THERMAL STORAGE OF HEAT. AVOID BLOCKING PATH OF SUN.	PREFERRED FOR WINTER SOLAR REFLECTION AND AS A THERMAL STORAGE OF HEAT. USE TO SHADE IN SUMMER.	AVOID INCREASED HEAT BUILD-UP DUE TO REFLECTION. USE FOR SUMMER SHADING.	AVOID INCREASED HEAT BUILD-UP DUE TO REFLECTION. USE FOR SHADING. USE IT'S THERMAL PROPERTIES AS A NIGHT TIME HEAT SOURCE.
	WIND	USE AS A WIND BREAK.	USE AS A WIND BREAK IN WINTER AND TO CHANNEL WINDS TO BUILDING IN SUMMER.	AVOID BLOCKING PREVAILING WINDS, USE TO CHANNEL WINDS TO BUILDING.	USE TO CHANNEL PREVAILING BREEZES TO BUILDING.
BODIES OF MATTER	SUN	PREFERRED TO SOUTH FOR ADDITIONAL REFLECTION OF SOLAR INSOLATION.	PREFERRED TO SOUTH FOR ADDITIONAL REFLECTION OF SOLAR INSOLATION.	AVOID BODIES OF WATER TO SOUTH AND ADDITIONAL HEAT BUILD-UP.	AVOID BODIES OF WATER TO SOUTH AND ADDITIONAL HEAT BUILD-UP.
	WIND	AVOID BODIES OF WATER IN PATH OF PREVAILING WINDS.	AVOID BODIES OF WATER IN PATH OF WINTER WINDS, PREFERRED LOCATION OF BODIES OF WATER IN PATH OF SUMMER BREEZES.		WATER PREFERRED ANYWHERE NEAR BUILDING FOR COOLING.

NATURAL ELEMENTS CONIFEROUS VEGETATION	COOL	TEMPERATE	HOT-HUMID	HOT-ARID
SUN	ALLOW PASSAGE OF SUN.	AVOID PLACEMENT TO SOUTH	ALLOW PASSAGE OF SUN.	OVERHANG BUILDING FOR SHADE.
WIND	USE TO PROTECT BUILDING FROM PREVAILING WINDS.	USE TO PROTECT BUILDING FROM WINTER WINDS. AVOID BLOCKING SUMMER BREEZES.	USE TO PROTECT BUILDING FROM WINTER WINDS. AVOID BLOCKING SUMMER BREEZES.	AVOID BLOCKING PREVAILING WINDS.

LIVING ROOM

			COOL	TEMPERATE	HOT-HUMID	HOT-ARID
ORIENTATION		LIGHT	S.SE TO SW	SE TO W.SW	E.NE TO NW	E.NE TO NW
		VENT	AVOID WINTER WINDS.	TOWARDS SUMMER WINDS. AVOID WINTER WINDS.	TOWARDS SUMMER WINDS.	TOWARDS SUMMER WINDS.
		HUMIDITY		TOWARDS PREVAILING SUMMER BREEZES.	TOWARDS PREVAILING BREEZES.	WIND PASSAGE OVER WATER FOR COOLING.
CONFIGURATION		LIGHT	E-W AXIS. LARGE OPENINGS. CLOSE RELATIONSHIP TO DAILY LIVING SPACES. AVERAGE CEILING HEIGHT.	E-W AXIS. LARGE OPENING WITH CAPACITY FOR SUMMER SHADING. CLOSE RELATIONSHIP TO DAILY LIVING SPACES. AVERAGE CEILING HEIGHT.	N-S AXIS OR E-W AXIS WITH SOLAR SHADING CAPABILITY. LARGE OPENING IF PROTECTED. AVERAGE OTHERWISE. OPEN RELATIONSHIP TO DAILY LIVING SPACES. HIGH CEILING HEIGHT.	N-S OR E-W AXIS WITH THICK THERMAL WALLS. SMALL OPENING HIGH IN WALL. CLOSE RELATIONSHIP TO DAILY LIVING SPACES. AVERAGE CEILING HEIGHT.
		VENT	PARALLEL AXIS TO PREVAILING WINDS. SMALL OPENINGS. COMPACT PLAN. AVERAGE CEILING HEIGHT.	PARALLEL AXIS TO WINTER WINDS, PERPENDICULAR AXIS TO SUMMER WINDS. AVERAGE OPENING. COMPACT PLAN. AVERAGE CEILING HEIGHT.	PERPENDICULAR TO PREVAILING WINDS. LARGE OPENINGS. OPEN PLAN. HIGH CEILING HEIGHT.	PERPENDICULAR TO PREVAILING WINDS. LARGE OPENINGS. OPEN PLAN. HIGH CEILING HEIGHT.

		COOL	TEMPERATE	HOT-HUMID	HOT-ARID
KITCHEN	ORIENTATION				
	LIGHT	E.SE TO W.NW	NW TO E	NW TO E.SE	NW TO SE
	VENT	TOWARDS SUMMER WIND.	TOWARDS SUMMER WIND	TOWARDS SUMMER WIND.	TOWARDS SUMMER WIND
	HUMIDITY		TOWARDS SUMMER WIND.	TOWARDS SUMMER WIND.	TOWARDS PREVAILING.
	CONFIGURATION				
	LIGHT	N-S AXIS. SMALL OPEN-ING. KITCHEN SHOULD BE CENTRALLY LOCATED. AVERAGE CEILING HEIGHT.	N-S AXIS. SMALL OPEN-ING. KITCHEN SHOULD BE CENTRALLY LOCATED. AVERAGE CEILING HEIGHT.	E-W AXIS. LARGE OPEN-INGS. KITCHEN TO BE LO-CATED APART FROM DAILY LIVING SPACES TO AVOID HEAT TRANSFER TO THOSE SPACES. HIGH CEILING HEIGHT.	E-W AXIS. LARGE OPEN-INGS. KITCHEN TO BE LO-CATED APART FROM DAILY LIVING SPACES TO AVOID HEAT TRANSFER TO THOSE SPACES. HIGH CEILING HEIGHT.
	VENT	N-S AXIS. SMALL OPEN-ING. COMPACT LAYOUT. LOW CEILING HEIGHT.	E-W AXIS. SMALL OPEN-ING. COMPACT LAYOUT. AVERAGE CEILING HEIGHT.	NW-SE AXIS. LARGE OPEN-INGS. OPEN PLAN. AVER-AGE CEILING HEIGHT.	N-S AXIS. LARGE OPEN-ING. OPEN PLAN. HIGH CEILING HEIGHT.

BUILDING INTERIOR

BATHROOM					
CONFIGURATION		ORIENTATION			
VENT	LIGHT	VENT	LIGHT		
				COOL	
PARALLEL TO PREVAILING WINDS. SMALL OPENING. COMPACT PLAN. LOW CEILING HEIGHT.	N-S AXIS. SMALL OPENING. CENTRALLY LOCATED. LOW CEILING HEIGHT.		NW TO E	COOL	
PARALLEL TO PREVAILING WINDS. SMALL OPENING. COMPACT PLAN. LOW CEILING HEIGHT.	N-S AXIS. SMALL OPENING. CENTRALLY LOCATED. LOW CEILING HEIGHT.		NW TO E	TEMPERATE	
PERPENDICULAR TO PREVAILING WINDS. MEDIUM OPENING. OPEN LAYOUT. AVERAGE CEILING HEIGHT.	N-S AXIS. MEDIUM OPENING. SEPARATED FROM DAILY LIVING SPACES WITH ACCESS. AVERAGE CEILING HEIGHT.	AVOID INTERFERENCE WITH PREVAILING WINDS.	SW TO NE	HOT-HUMID	
PERPENDICULAR TO PREVAILING WINDS. MEDIUM OPENING. COMPACT PLAN. LOW CEILING HEIGHT.	N-S AXIS. SMALL OPENING. SEPARATED FROM DAILY LIVING SPACES WITH DIRECT ACCESS. LOW CEILING HEIGHT.	AVOID INTERFERENCE. WITH PREVAILING WINDS.	SW TO NE	HOT-ARID	

BEDROOM		COOL	TEMPERATE	HOT-HUMID	HOT-ARID
ORIENTATION	LIGHT	NE TO SE	NE TO SE	NW TO SE	NE TO SE
	VENT	PROTECT FROM WINTER WINDS.	PROTECT FROM WINTER WINDS. EXPOSE TO SUMMER BREEZES.	ORIENT TO NIGHT BREEZES.	ORIENT TO CAPTURE PREVAILING BREEZES.
CONFIGURATION	LIGHT	N-S AXIS. SMALL OPENING. SEPARATED FROM DAILY LIVING SPACES FOR PRIVACY. LOW CEILING HEIGHT.	N-S AXIS. SMALL OPENING. SEPARATE FROM DAILY LIVING SPACES FOR PRIVACY. LOW CEILING HEIGHT.	N-S AXIS. LARGE OPENING. SEPARATED FROM DAILY LIVING SPACES WITHIN OPEN PLAN. AVERAGE CEILING HEIGHT.	N-S AXIS. MEDIUM OPENING. SEPARATED FROM DAILY LIVING SPACES WITHIN COMPACT PLAN. LOW CEILING HEIGHT.
	VENT	PARALLEL TO PREVAILING WINDS. SMALL OPENING. COMPACT PLAN. LOW CEILING HEIGHT.	PARALLEL TO WINTER WIND. PERPENDICULAR TO SUMMER BREEZES. SMALL OPENINGS. COMPACT PLAN. LOW CEILING HEIGHT.	PERPENDICULAR TO NIGHT BREEZES. LARGE OPENING. OPEN PLAN. AVERAGE CEILING HEIGHT.	PERPENDICULAR TO PREVAILING WINDS. SMALL OPENINGS. COMPACT PLAN. LOW CEILING HEIGHT.

BUILDING INTERIOR

		COOL	TEMPERATE	HOT-HUMID	HOT-ARID
ENTRANCE					
ORIENTATION	LIGHT	SW TO SE	W.SW TO E.SE	SW TO NE	NW TO E
	VENT	PROTECTED FROM PREVAILING WINDS.	PROTECTED FROM WINTER WINDS.	PROTECTED FROM WINTER WINDS AND IN DIRECT PATH OF SUMMER WIND.	ORIENT TO CAPTURE AND FUNNEL PREVAILING WINDS THROUGH BUILDING.
CONFIGURATION	LIGHT	PERPENDICULAR TO STRONGEST SUN. LARGE OPENING FOR SOLAR HEAT GAIN. VESTIBULE SPACE BEFORE ENTERING LIVING SPACES.	PERPENDICULAR TO STRONGEST SUN. LARGE OPENING FOR SOLAR HEAT GAIN. VESTIBULE SPACE BEFORE ENTERING LIVING SPACES.	PARALLEL TO STRONGEST SUN. AVERAGE OPENING PROTECTED FROM SUN. DIRECT ENTRANCE TO LIVING SPACES.	PARALLEL TO STRONGEST SUN. SMALL OPENING PROTECTED FROM SUN. VESTIBULE SPACE BEFORE ENTERING LIVING SPACE.
	VENT	PARALLEL TO PREVAILING WINDS. SMALL OPENING. COMPACT PLAN.	PARALLEL TO WINTER WINDS. PERPENDICULAR TO SUMMER BREEZES. SMALL OPENING, COMPACT PLAN.	PERPENDICULAR TO PREVAILING WINDS. LARGE OPENING. OPEN LAYOUT.	PERPENDICULAR TO PREVAILING WINDS. MEDIUM OPENING. COMPACT PLAN.

		COOL	TEMPERATE	HOT-HUMID	HOT-ARID
ORIENTATION	LIGHT	NW TO NE	NW TO NE	W TO NE	S.SE TO NW
	VENT	EXTERIOR SURFACE TOWARD WINTER WIND TO ACT AS BUFFER.	TOWARD WINTER WIND TO ACT AS BUFFER. AVOID BLOCKING SUMMER BREEZES.	ORIENT TO BLOCK WINTER WIND AND ALLOW PASSAGE OF SUMMER BREEZES.	AVOID BLOCKING SUMMER BREEZES.
CONFIGURATION	LIGHT	DIRECT SUN NOT NEEDED. SMALL OPENING, PERIPHAL OF LIVING SPACES. LOW CEILING HEIGHT.	DIRECT SUN NOT NEEDED. SMALL OPENING. OF LIVING SPACES. LOW CEILING HEIGHT.	DIRECT SUN NOT NEEDED. AVERAGE OPENING. SEPARATED FROM DAILY LIVING SPACES. AVERAGE CEILING HEIGHT.	DIRECT SUN NOT NEEDED. SMALL OPENING. SEPARATED FROM DAILY LIVING SPACES. LOW CEILING HEIGHT.
	VENT	PERPENDICULAR TO PREVAILING WINDS TO ACT AS A BUFFER. SMALL OPENING. COMPACT PLAN.	PERPENDICULAR TO PREVAILING WINDS TO ACT AS A BUFFER. SMALL OPENING. COMPACT PLAN.	PARALLEL TO PREVAILING WINDS TO AVOID BLOCKING VENTILATION. AVERAGE OPENING. OPEN LAYOUT.	PARALLEL TO PREVAILING WINDS TO ALLOW COOL WINDS TO STRIKE THE BUILDING. SMALL OPENING. COMPACT PLAN.
STORAGE					

BUILDING INTERIOR

GARAGE				
		COOL	TEMPERATE	HOT-HUMID	HOT-ARID

ORIENTATION	COOL	TEMPERATE	HOT-HUMID	HOT-ARID
LIGHT	NW TO NE	NW TO NE	NW TO NE	N
VENT	PLACED TO PROTECT STRUCTURE FROM PREVAILING WINDS.	PLACED TO PROTECT STRUCTURE FROM WINTER WIND AND ALLOW SUMMER BREEZES TO STRIKE BUILDING.	AVOID BLOCKING PREVAILING WINDS FROM STRIKING BUILDING.	AVOID BLOCKING PREVAILING WINDS FROM STRIKING BUILDING.

CONFIGURATION	COOL	TEMPERATE	HOT-HUMID	HOT-ARID
LIGHT	DIRECT SUN NOT NEEDED. GARAGE DOOR TO S-SW. ATTACHED TO STRUCTURE.	DIRECT SUN NOT NEEDED. GARAGE DOOR TO S-SW. ATTACHED TO STRUCTURE.	DIRECT SUN NOT NEEDED. AVOID GARAGE DOOR TO SOUTH. DETACHED FROM STRUCTURE.	DIRECT SUN NOT NEEDED. AVOID GARAGE DOOR TO SOUTH. DETACHED FROM STRUCTURE.
VENT	PERPENDICULAR TO PREVAILING WINDS TO ACT AS BUFFER. COMPACT PLAN. SMALL OPENING.	PERPENDICULAR TO WINTER WINDS TO ACT AS BUFFER. AVOID BLOCKING SUMMER BREEZES. COMPACT PLAN. SMALL OPENING.	PARALLEL TO PREVAILING WINDS TO AVOID BLOCKING VENTILATION. AVERAGE OPENING. OPEN LAYOUT.	PARALLEL TO PREVAILING WINDS TO AVOID BLOCKING VENTILATION. SMALL OPENING. COMPACT LAYOUT.

		COOL	TEMPERATE	HOT-HUMID	HOT-ARID
EXTERIOR WALL	THERMAL	LARGE THERMAL MASS WITH HEAVY INSULATION TO OUTSIDE TO IMPROVE HEAT STORAGE.	LARGE THERMAL MASS WITH HEAVY INSULATION TO OUTSIDE TO IMPROVE HEAT STORAGE.		MASS ON OUTER WALLS WITH INSULATION TO INSIDE.
	INFILTRATION	MINIMIZE INFILTRATION WITH PROPER INSULATION, WEATHERSTRIPPING, AND CAULKING. REDUCE PERCENTAGE OF WALL OPENINGS EXPOSED TO PREVAILING WINDS.	MINIMIZE INFILTRATION WITH PROPER INSULATION, WEATHERSTRIPPING, AND CAULKING. REDUCE PERCENTAGE OF WALL OPENINGS EXPOSED TO PREVAILING WINDS.	MAXIMIZE INFILTRATION AND AIR VENTILATION WITH LARGE PERCENTAGE OF OPENINGS EXPOSED TO PREVAILING WINDS.	MINIMIZE INFILTRATION WITH PROPER INSULATION, WEATHERSTRIPPING AND CAULKING. MAXIMIZE VENTILATION WITH LARGE PERCENTAGE OF WALL OPENINGS EXPOSED TO PREVAILING WINDS.
	MOISTURE	MOISTURE BARRIER PLACED ON INNER SURFACE OF EXTERIOR CONSTRUCTION.	MOISTURE BARRIER PLACED ON INNER SURFACE OF EXTERIOR CONSTRUCTION.	MOISTURE BARRIER PLACED ON OUTER SURFACE OF EXTERIOR CONSTRUCTION.	MOISTURE BARRIER PLACED ON OUTER SURFACE OF EXTERIOR CONSTRUCTION.
ROOF	THERMAL	ORIENT TO ABSORB SUN. DARKENED COLOR TO INCREASE ABSORPTION.	ORIENT TO ABSORB SUN. DARKENED COLOR TO INCREASE ABSORPTION.		ORIENT SO AS NOT TO ABSORB SUN. LIGHT COLORED TO REFLECT SUN.
	INFILTRATION	SLOPED TO DEFLECT WIND.	SLOPED TO DEFLECT WIND.	FLAT WITH OVERHANG TO CAPTURE WIND.	FLAT WITH OVERHANG TO CAPTURE WIND.
	MOISTURE	POSITIONED TO COLLECT SNOW. VAPOR BARRIER PLACED ON INNER SURFACE OF ROOF.	POSITIONED TO COLLECT SNOW. VAPOR BARRIER PLACED ON INNER SURFACE OF ROOF.		POSITIONED TO COLLECT RAINWATER. VAPOR BARRIER PLACED ON OUTER SURFACE OF ROOF.

BUILDING COMPONENT

		COOL	TEMPERATE	HOT-HUMID	HOT-ARID
WINDOWS	THERMAL	MINIMIZE WINDOW AREA FACING PREVAILING WINDS AND TAKE ADVANTAGE OF SOLAR HEAT GAIN TO SOUTH. UTILIZE TRIPLE GLAZING. UTILIZE THERMAL SHUTTERS	MINIMIZE WINDOW AREA FACING WINTER WINDS AND TAKE ADVANTAGE OF SOLAR HEAT GAIN TO SOUTH. EXPOSE WINDOWS TO BREEZES AND SHADE FROM DIRECT SUN IN SUMMER. UTILIZE DOUBLE GLAZING.	MINIMIZE DIRECT SUN ON WINDOWS AND EXPOSE TO PREVAILING WINDS. MAXIMIZE GLASS AREA.	MINIMIZE DIRECT SUN ON WINDOWS AND EXPOSE TO PREVAILING WINDS. MINIMIZE GLASS AREA. UTILIZE DOUBLE GLAZING.
	INFILTRATION	USE SEALED WINDOWS. USE FIXED GLASS. MINIMIZE GLASS AREA EXPOSED TO PREVAILING WINDS.	USE OPERABLE WINDOWS WITH SEALING GASKETS AND CAM LATCHES. MINIMIZE WINDOWS EXPOSED TO WINTER WINDS.	USE OPERABLE WINDOWS FOR OPTION OF OPENING UP TO PREVAILING WINDS. AND CAM LATCHES. USE LARGE AMOUNTS OF GLASS EXPOSED TO PREVAILING WINDS.	USE OPERABLE WINDOWS WITH SEALING GASKETS AND CAM LATCHES. MAXIMIZE WINDOW EXPOSURE TOWARDS PREVAILING WINDS.
DOORS	THERMAL	ORIENT TOWARD SUN.	ORIENT TOWARD WINTER SUN AND SHADE FROM SUMMER SUN.	PROTECT FROM DIRECT SUN.	ORIENT TO NORTH AWAY FROM HEAT BUILD-UP.
	INFILTRATION	PROTECT FROM PREVAILING WINDS	PROTECT FROM WINTER WINDS AND EXPOSE TO SUMMER BREEZES.	ORIENT TOWARDS PREVAILING WINDS.	ORIENT TOWARDS PREVAILING WINDS.

EXTERIOR SOLAR CONTROLS	COOL	TEMPERATE	HOT-HUMID	HOT-ARID
THERMAL	AVOID SHADING DEVICES. DARK COLORED ABSORPTIVE SURFACES PREFERRED TO INCREASE SOLAR INSOLATION	USE SOLAR CONTROLS SUCH AS LOUVERS AND OVERHANGS POSITIONED TO ADMIT WINTER SUN AND BLOCK SUMMER SUN.	USE SOLAR CONTROLS SUCH AS LOUVERS, OVERHANGS AND BUILDING FACADES TO SHADE BUILDING.	SOLAR CONTROLS SUCH AS LOUVERS, OVERHANGS, AND BUILDING FACADES DESIRED TO MAXIMIZE SHADE. AVOID REFLECTIVE SURFACES THAT CAUSE ADDITIONAL HEAT GAIN.
INFILTRATION	AVOID LOUVERS AND OVERHANGS FROM CAPTURING PREVAILING WINDS	AVOID SOLAR CONTROLS CAPTURING WINTER WINDS. OVERHANGS AND LOUVERS THAT CAPTURE SUMMER BREEZES ARE PREFERRED.	USE SOLAR CONTROLS TO CAPTURE PREVAILING WINDS FOR COOLING.	USE SOLAR CONTROLS TO CAPTURE PREVAILING WINDS FOR COOLING.
MOISTURE	OVERHANGS PROTECT WALLS AND GLAZING FROM PRECIPITATION.	OVERHANGS PROTECT WALLS AND GLAZING FROM PRECIPITATION.	OVERHANGS PROTECT WALLS AND GLAZING FROM PRECIPITATION.	OVERHANGS PROTECT WALLS AND GLAZING FROM PRECIPITATION.

BUILDING COMPONENT

INTERIOR SOLAR CONTROLS

	COOL	TEMPERATE	HOT-HUMID	HOT-ARID
THERMAL	AVOID BLINDS AND DRAPES BLOCKING SUN DURING DAY. CLOSE BLINDS AND DRAPES AT NIGHT TO RETAIN HEAT IN INTERIOR.	IN WINTER, AVOID HAVING BLINDS AND DRAPES BLOCK SUN DURING DAY. KEEP BLINDS AND DRAPES CLOSED AT NIGHT TO RETAIN HEAT. IN SUMMER, CLOSE BLINDS AND DRAPES DURING DAY AND OPEN AT NIGHT TO RELEASE HEAT.	KEEP BLINDS AND DRAPES CLOSED DURING DAY TO PREVENT HEAT BUILD-UP AND OPEN AT NIGHT TO RELEASE HEAT.	CLOSE BLINDS AND DRAPES DURING DAY TO PREVENT HEAT BUILD-UP AND OPEN THEM AT NIGHT TO RELEASE HEAT.
INFILTRATION	USE BLINDS AND DRAPES, PARTICULARLY TOWARD PREVAILING WINDS, TO RE-DUCE INFILTRATION.	IN WINTER, USE BLINDS AND DRAPES TO REDUCE INFILTRATION. IN SUMMER, DO NOT BLOCK BREEZES FOR IMPROVED VENTILATION.	EXTERIOR SHADING DE-VICES PREFERRED. IN-TERIOR SHADING DEVICES SHOULD BE FLEXIBLE TO ALLOW WINDOWS TO BE OPENED FOR VENTI-LATION.	AVOID BLOCKING PRE-VAILING WINDS WITH BLINDS AND DRAPES.

PART III

SOLAR ENERGY SYSTEMS

THE ENERGY REQUIREMENTS WHICH ARE NOT MET BY THE ENERGY CONSCIOUS DESIGN CAN BE SUP-PLIED THROUGH SOLAR ENERGY SYSTEMS. THESE CAN PROVIDE SPACE HEATING AND COOLING, DOMESTIC HOT WATER AND ELECTRICITY FOR OTHER USES.

THIS PART INTRODUCES THE USER TO THE PRINCIPLES INVOLVED IN THE DESIGN OF SOLAR SYSTEMS. A LIST ENUMERATING MANUFACTURERS OF SOLAR PRODUCTS IS PRESENTED IN APPENDIX D.

SECTION 8   PASSIVE SYSTEMS

PASSIVE SYSTEMS OPERATE ON THE BASIS OF RE-
DUCING ENERGY CONSUMPTION AS OPPOSED TO IN-
CREASING THE AMOUNT OF ENERGY SUPPLIED. PASS-
IVE SYSTEMS CAN BE DEFINED AS THE METHODS
AND TECHNIQUES USED FOR GATHERING AND CON-
SERVING ENERGY WHICH CONTAIN MINIMUM MECHAN-
IZED PARTS AND FORM AN INTEGRAL PART OF THE
BUILDING'S SPACE ENCLOSING ELEMENTS. IT IS BE-
CAUSE OF THE LAST REASON THAT THE COST OF
THEIR IMPLEMENTATION IS RELATIVELY LOW.

THE PRINCIPLE ILLUS-
TRATED IN FIGS. 8.1 AND
8.2 IS THAT OF HEAT
LAG.

DURING THE DAY THE
SUN HEATS THE EXTER-
IOR WALL AND ROOF.
AT NIGHT THE WALL
AND ROOF RELEASE
THIS HEAT TO THE IN-
TERIOR. THIS SYSTEM
IS RECOMMENDED FOR
REGIONS WITH LARGE
TEMPERATURE DIFFER-
ENTIALS.

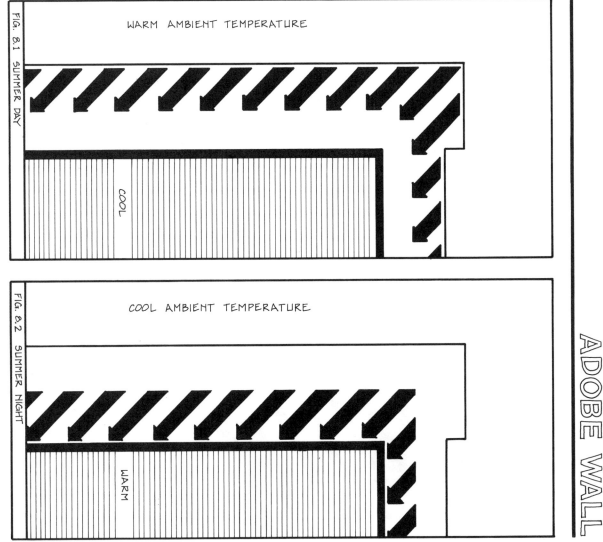

WARM AMBIENT TEMPERATURE

COOL

FIG. 8.1 SUMMER DAY

COOL AMBIENT TEMPERATURE

WARM

FIG. 8.2 SUMMER NIGHT

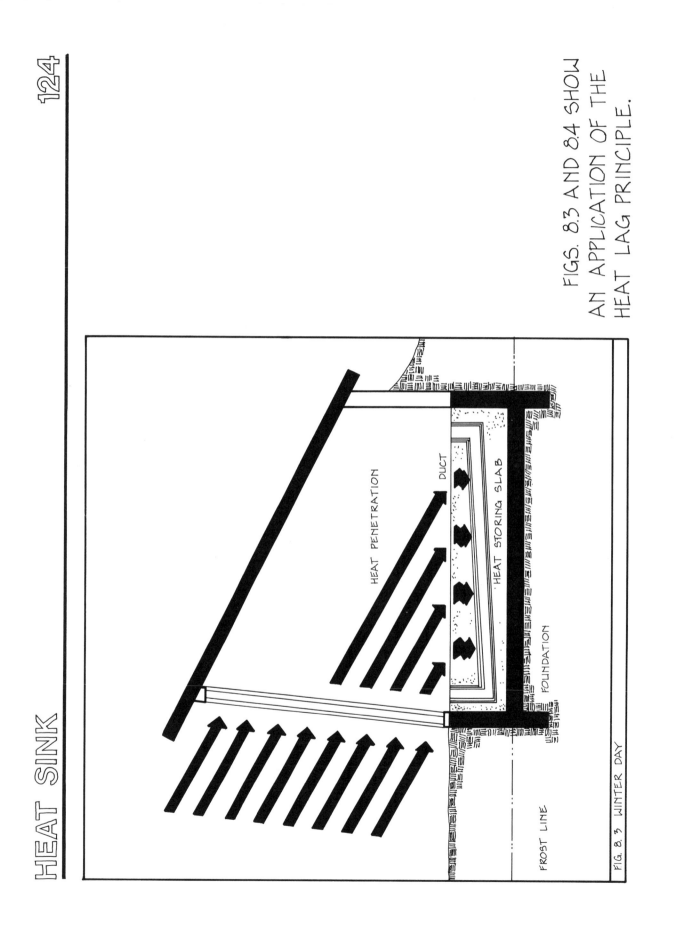

HEAT PENETRATION

DUCT

HEAT STORING SLAB

FOUNDATION

FROST LINE

FIG. 8.3 WINTER DAY

FIGS. 8.3 AND 8.4 SHOW AN APPLICATION OF THE HEAT LAG PRINCIPLE.

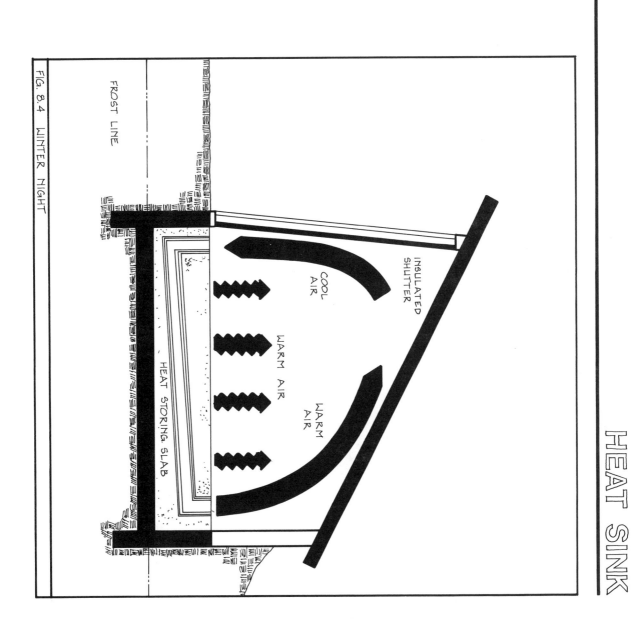

FIG. 8.4 WINTER NIGHT

FROST LINE

INSULATED SHUTTER

COOL AIR

WARM AIR

WARM AIR

HEAT STORING SLAB

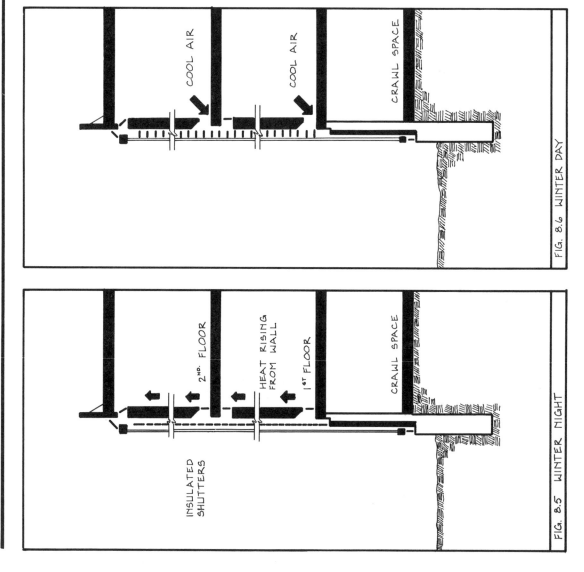

INSULATED
SHUTTERS

2ND. FLOOR

HEAT RISING
FROM WALL

1ST FLOOR

CRAWL SPACE

FIG. 8.5 WINTER NIGHT

COOL AIR

COOL AIR

CRAWL SPACE

FIG. 8.6 WINTER DAY

FIGS. 8.5 AND 8.6
ILLUSTRATE THE WINTER
OPERATING MODES OF THE
TROMBE WALL.

FIGS. 8.7 AND 8.8
ILLUSTRATE THE SUMMER
OPERATING MODES OF THE
TROMBE WALL.

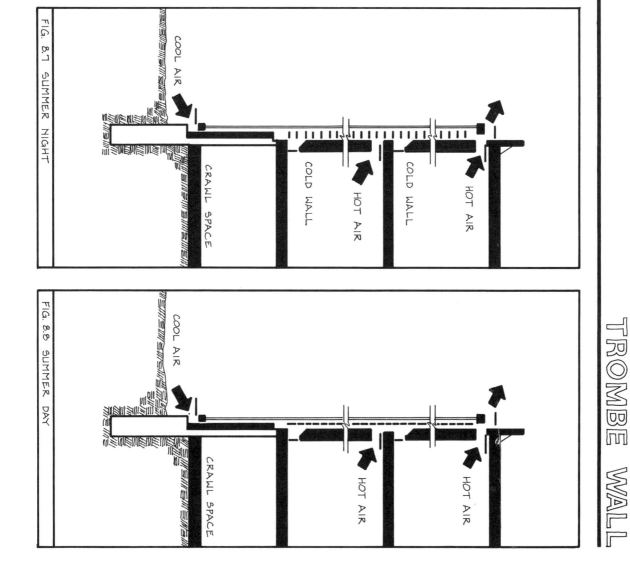

FIG. 8.7 SUMMER NIGHT

COOL AIR

CRAWL SPACE

COLD WALL

HOT AIR

COLD WALL

HOT AIR

FIG. 8.8 SUMMER DAY

COOL AIR

CRAWL SPACE

HOT AIR

HOT AIR

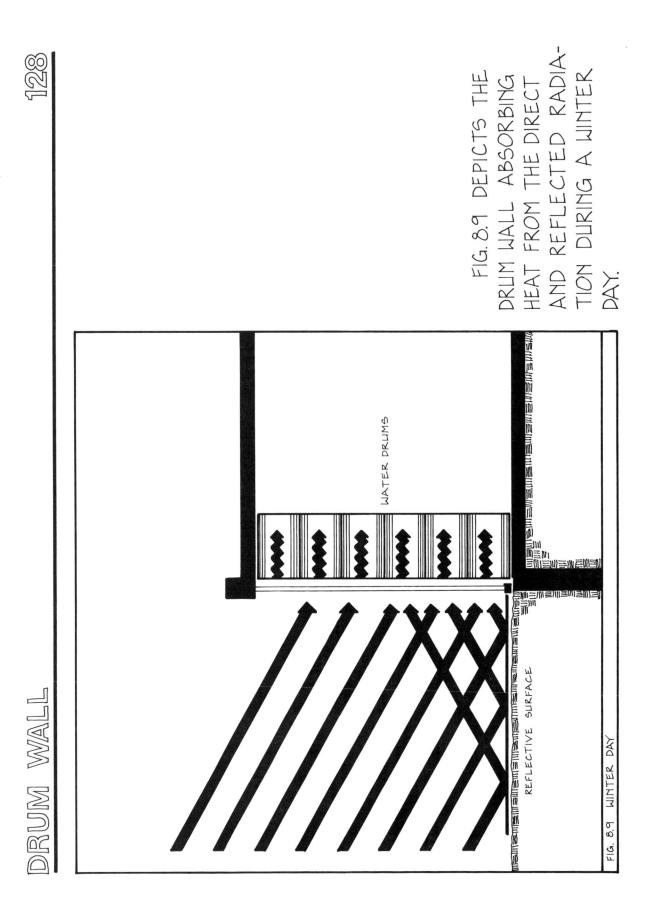

WATER DRUMS

REFLECTIVE SURFACE

FIG. 8.9 WINTER DAY

FIG. 8.9 DEPICTS THE DRUM WALL ABSORBING HEAT FROM THE DIRECT AND REFLECTED RADIATION DURING A WINTER DAY.

DRUM WALL

FIG. 8.10 ILLUSTRATES
THE DRUM WALL RADIAT-
ING HEAT INTO THE
LIVING SPACE DURING A
WINTER NIGHT.

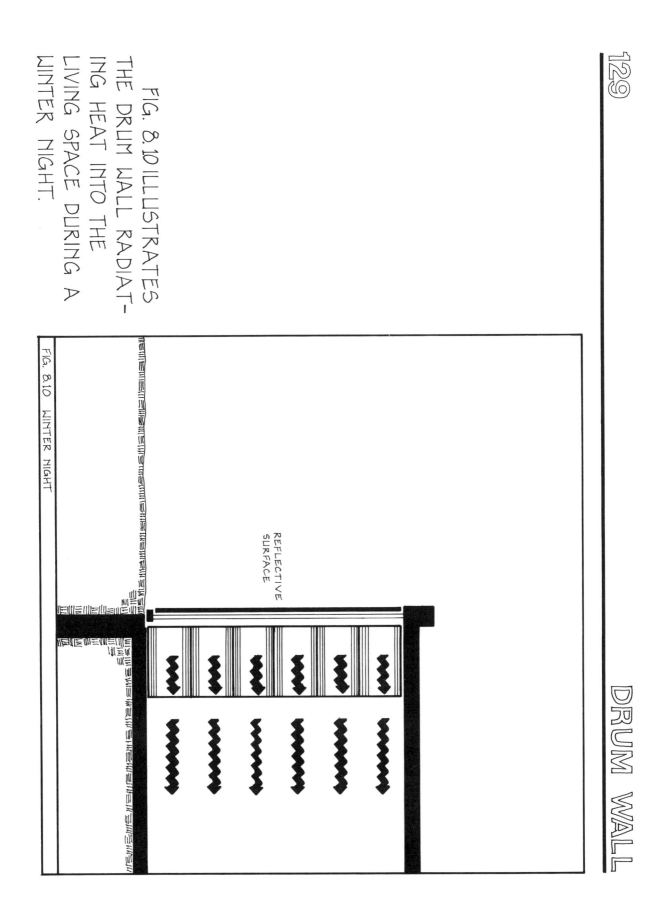

FIG. 8.10   WINTER NIGHT

REFLECTIVE
SURFACE

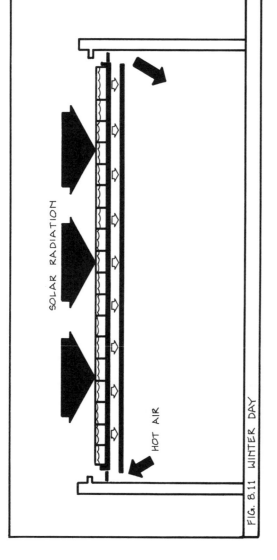

SOLAR RADIATION

HOT AIR

FIG. 8.11 WINTER DAY

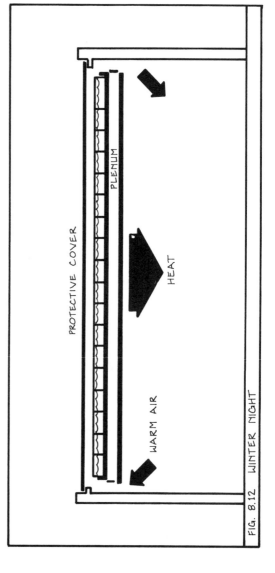

PROTECTIVE COVER

PLENUM

HEAT

WARM AIR

FIG. 8.12 WINTER NIGHT

FIG. 8.11 ILLUSTRATES
THE OPERATING MODE FOR
A WINTER DAY. AS THE
WATER BAGS ARE HEATED
BY THE SOLAR RADIATION
THEY RERADIATE THE
HEAT INTO THE PLENUM.

IN THE SUMMER, THE
ROOF POND CAN BE
USED AS A COOLING
SYSTEM.

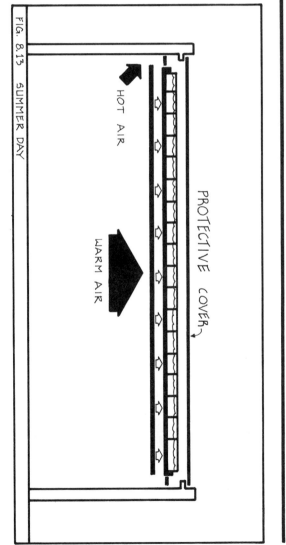

FIG. 8.13 SUMMER DAY

HOT AIR

PROTECTIVE COVER

WARM AIR

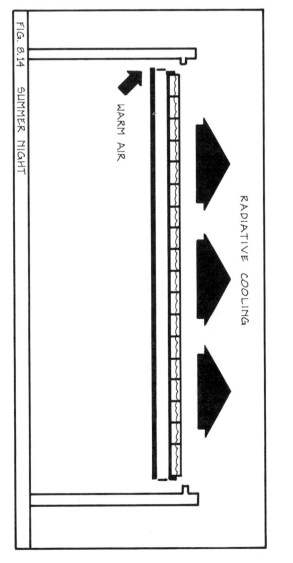

FIG. 8.14 SUMMER NIGHT

WARM AIR

RADIATIVE COOLING

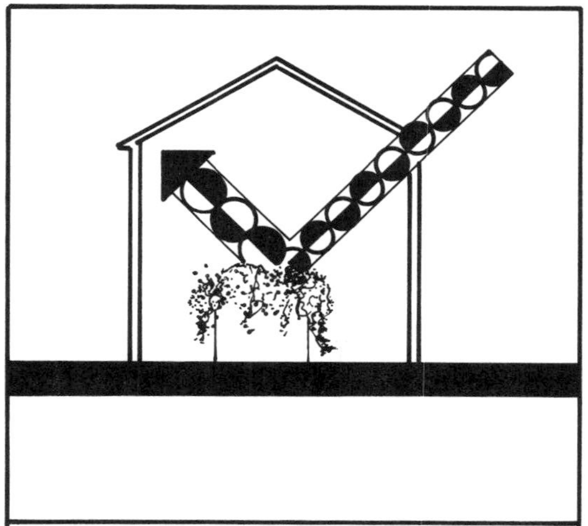

GLASS IS TRANSPARENT TO SHORTWAVE SOLAR RADIATION. THE RADIATION REFLECTED FROM THE PLANT HAS A LONGWAVE CHARACTERISTIC. GLASS IS OPAQUE TO THIS TYPE OF RADIATION. MAXIMUM RADIATION PENETRATION OCCURS WHEN THE ANGLE OF INCIDENCE IS 90°. THIS TAKES PLACE ONCE A DAY WITH NORMAL GLAZING AND TWICE A DAY WHEN RIDGE GLAZING IS USED. THE SAME PRINCIPLE SHOULD BE APPLIED WHEN DESIGNING COLLECTOR COVERS AND HEAT SINK WALLS.

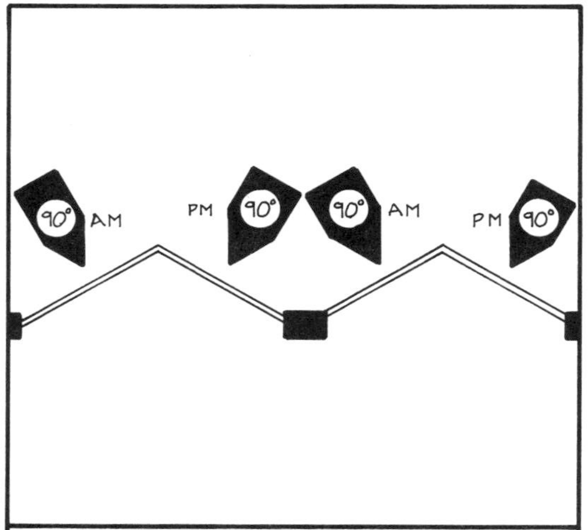

FIG. 8.15 GREENHOUSE EFFECT

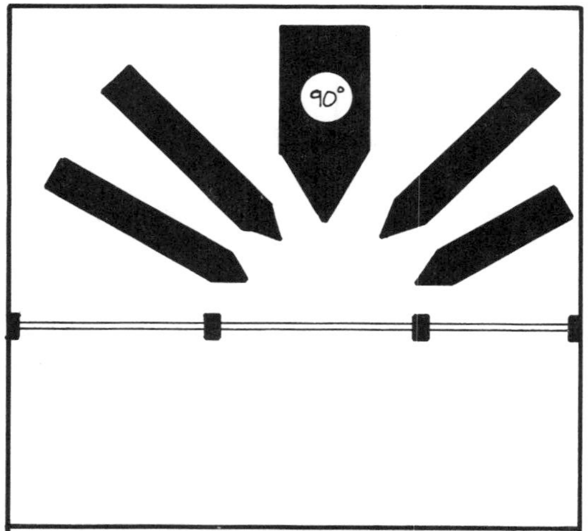

FIG. 8.17 RIDGE GLAZING

FIG. 8.16 NORMAL GLAZING

THE ADDITION OF RE-
FLECTORS AROUND THE
GREENHOUSE WILL IN-
CREASE THE AMOUNT OF
SOLAR RADIATION IT
ABSORBS. AT NIGHT OR
ON A CLOUDY DAY THE
GREENHOUSE WILL LOSE
HEAT TO THE SURROUND-
ING AMBIENT. THIS CAN
BE CONTROLLED
THROUGH THE USE OF
SHADES AND/OR BEAD
WALLS.

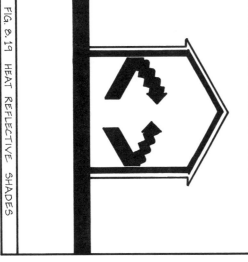

FIG. 8.19 HEAT REFLECTIVE SHADES

FIG. 8.18 GREENHOUSE REFLECTORS

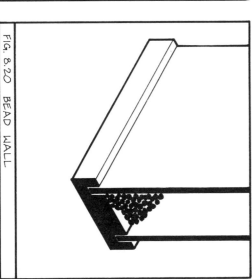

FIG. 8.20 BEAD WALL

ACTIVE SOLAR ENERGY SYSTEMS CONSIST OF
SIX ELEMENTS: COLLECTOR, TRANSPORT, STORAGE,
DISTRIBUTION, BACK-UP ELEMENT AND CONTROLS.
THERE ARE INSTANCES WHERE VARIOUS ELEMENTS
ARE COMBINED INTO ONE COMPONENT. THE SYSTEM'S
OPERATING MODE CAN BE DESCRIBED IN THE
FOLLOWING MANNER: SOLAR RADIATION IS GATH-
ERED BY THE COLLECTOR, TRANSPORTED TO THE
STORAGE UNIT, DELIVERED TO THE LIVING SPACE
AND MONITORED THROUGH THE CONTROLS. THE
BACK-UP, OR AUXILIARY ELEMENT PROVIDES
ENERGY WHEN THE STORAGE UNIT DOES NOT CON-
TAIN SUFFICIENT ENERGY OF ITS OWN.

COLLECTORS

A COLLECTOR IS DEFINED AS THE ELEMENT WHICH CONVERTS INCIDENT SOLAR RADIATION INTO USABLE ENERGY. THIS ENERGY CAN BE THERMAL OR ELECTRICAL. COLLECTORS CAN BE CATEGORIZED AS FOCUSING OR NON-FOCUSING. FOCUSING COLLECTORS CONCENTRATE THE SOLAR RADIATION PRIOR TO ITS BEING ABSORBED. NON-FOCUSING COLLECTORS ABSORB THE RADIATION AT THE SAME DENSITY AS IT IS RECEIVED BY THE EARTH'S SURFACE.

A FLAT-PLATE, OR NON-FOCUSING, COLLECTOR CONSISTS OF AN ABSORBING PLATE WHICH CAN BE FLAT, CORRUGATED OR GROOVED. THE ABSORBING PLATE IS GENERALLY TREATED TO INCREASE SOLAR RADIATION ABSORPTION. THE BEST ABSORBING SURFACES IN ORDER OF DECREASING EFFICIENCY ARE: COATED SURFACES, TYLER SCREENS AND GRAPHITE.

THE COLLECTOR IS INSULATED IN THE BACK TO REDUCE HEAT LOSSES AND IT IS COVERED IN THE FRONT WITH ONE TO THREE SHEETS OF CLEAR MATERIAL. THESE TRAP HEAT WITHIN THE COLLECTOR AND MINIMIZE CONVECTIVE LOSSES.

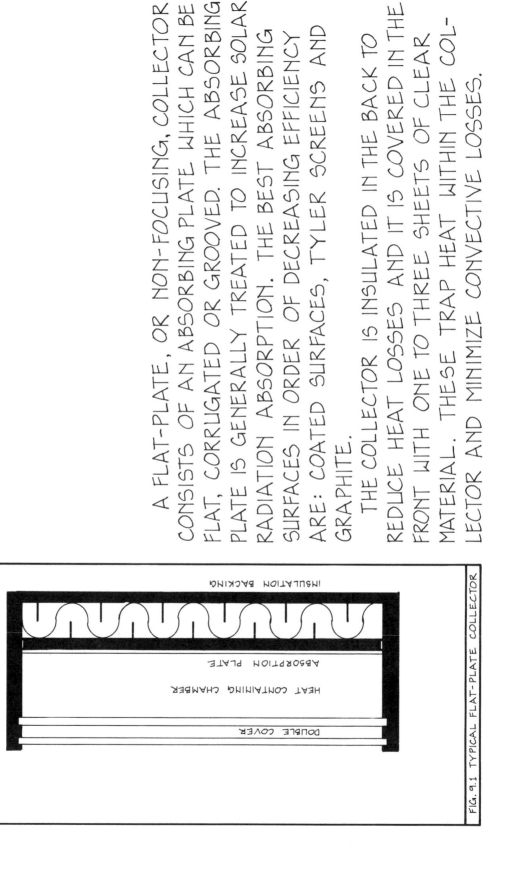

FIG. 9.1 TYPICAL FLAT-PLATE COLLECTOR

THE TRAPPED HEAT IS REMOVED FROM THE COLLEC-
TOR BY MEANS OF A HEAT EXCHANGE AGENT, SUCH
AS AIR, WATER, ANTI-FREEZE MIXTURE OR GASEOUS
MATERIAL. WHEN THE COLLECTOR USES AIR TO REMOVE
THE HEAT, IT IS CALLED AN AIR COOLED COLLECTOR.
IF IT USES WATER IT IS A WATER COOLED COLLECTOR.
WHEN THE HEAT REMOVING AGENT IS TOTALLY EN-
CLOSED IN THE PANEL OR TUBE, THE SYSTEM IS
SAID TO BE CLOSED. WHEN THE AGENT MOVES
FREELY BETWEEN THE ABSORBING PLATE AND THE
COVER SHEET, IT IS AN OPEN SYSTEM.

FIG. 9.3 CLOSED, WATER COOLED COLLECTOR

WATER INTAKE

WATER OUTPUT

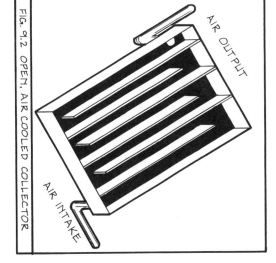

FIG. 9.2 OPEN, AIR COOLED COLLECTOR

AIR OUTPUT

AIR INTAKE

ALTHOUGH FLAT-PLATE COLLECTORS ABSORB BOTH DIRECT AND DIFFUSE RADIATION, IT IS ESSENTIAL TO THE SYSTEMS EFFICIENCY TO MAXIMIZE THE COLLECTION OF DIRECT RADIATION. THIS IS ACHIEVED THROUGH PROPER ORIENTATION AND INCLINATION OF THE COLLECTOR. FOR SPACE HEATING THE INCLINATION IS THE LATITUDE PLUS 15°. FOR SPACE HEATING AND COOLING THE INCLINATION SHOULD BE LATITUDE PLUS 5°. FOR BOTH THESE APPLICATIONS, THE ORIENTATION SHOULD BE FROM TRUE SOUTH TO SOUTHWEST. ANOTHER WAY TO INCREASE THE COLLECTOR'S EFFICIENCY IS TO USE REFLECTIVE PANELS.

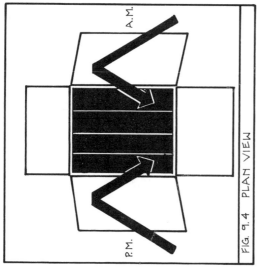

FIG. 9.4 PLAN VIEW

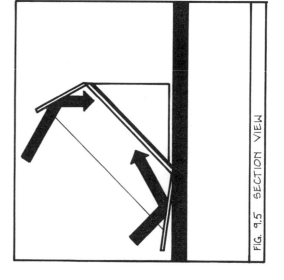

FIG. 9.5 SECTION VIEW

FIGS. 9.6 THROUGH
9.11 ILLUSTRATE VARI-
OUS TYPES OF ABSORB-
ING PLATES USED IN
THE CONSTRUCTION OF
FLAT-PLATE COLLECTORS.
IT IS IMPORTANT TO NOTE
THAT THE "HEADER"
SHOULD HAVE A CROSS-
SECTIONAL AREA EQUAL
TO OR LARGER THAN
THE SUM OF THE AREAS
OF THE INDIVIDUAL
CHANNELS.

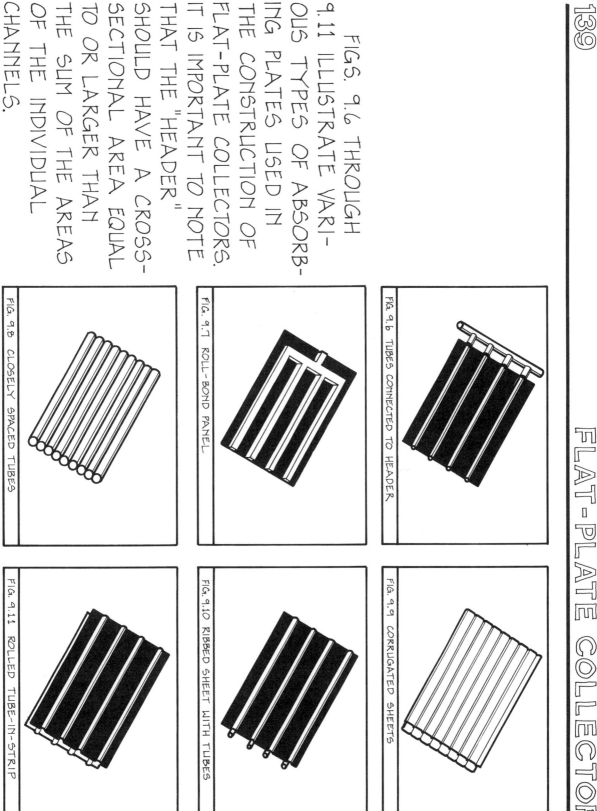

FIG. 9.6 TUBES CONNECTED TO HEADER

FIG. 9.7 ROLL-BOND PANEL

FIG. 9.8 CLOSELY SPACED TUBES

FIG. 9.9 CORRUGATED SHEETS

FIG. 9.10 RIBBED SHEET WITH TUBES

FIG. 9.11 ROLLED TUBE-IN-STRIP

FIG. 9.12 ABSORBING PLATE

FIG. 9.13 REFLECTOR

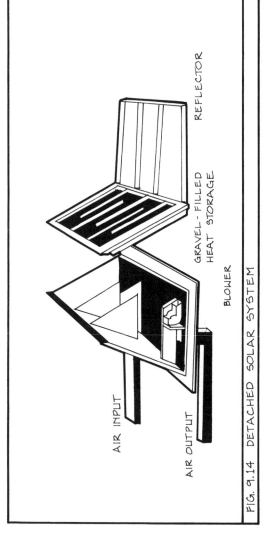

REFLECTOR

GRAVEL-FILLED
HEAT STORAGE

BLOWER

AIR INPUT

AIR OUTPUT

FIG. 9.14 DETACHED SOLAR SYSTEM

FIGS. 9.12 THROUGH 9.14 ILLUSTRATE THE ENERGY KING T.M. SOLAR SYSTEM.

FLAT-PLATE COLLECTOR

FIGS. 9.15 AND 9.16 ILLUSTRATE A HOME-MADE COLLECTOR WITH AN INTEGRATED STORAGE SYSTEM. THIS TYPE OF SYSTEM IS BEST SUITED FOR SMALL RETROFIT-TING PROJECTS.

INSTRUCTIONS

A. CUT 2-2×10'S FOR TOP AND BOT-TOM PLATES. MARK 16" O.C. FOR STUDS.

B. CUT 4-2×10'S, 7'-9" LONG FOR STUDS. CUT 10"× 8" OPENING NEAR ONE END FOR AIR PASSAGE.

C. SPACE STUDS AT 16" CENTERS WITH ALTERNATING OPENINGS AS SHOWN.

D. NAIL PLYWOOD ON TOP OF FRAME WITH 4d COMMON NAILS.

E. AT END MODULES ONLY: CUT 10" DIA. HOLE FOR CONNECTION TO SUPPLY OR RETURN AIR DUCTS.

F. CUT PIECES OF 1½" THICK STYRO-FOAM INSULATION TO FIT EACH SPACE BETWEEN STUDS. GLUE TO PLYWOOD BACK WITH STYROFOAM.

G. CUT MORE PIECES OF 1½" THICK STYROFOAM FOR ALL EDGES EXPOS-ED TO COLD. GLUE TO 2×10'S WITH SAME MASTIC.

H. PAINT EVERYTHING, (INSIDE, OUT-SIDE, BACK) WITH FLAT BLACK PAINT.

I. TACK A 4'×8' SHEET OF "SUN-LITE" SOLAR COLLECTOR MATERIAL OVER CAULKED 1×2'S WITH GALVANIZED ROOFING NAILS.

J. RUN A BEAD OF CAULKING OVER ALL NAILED AREAS.

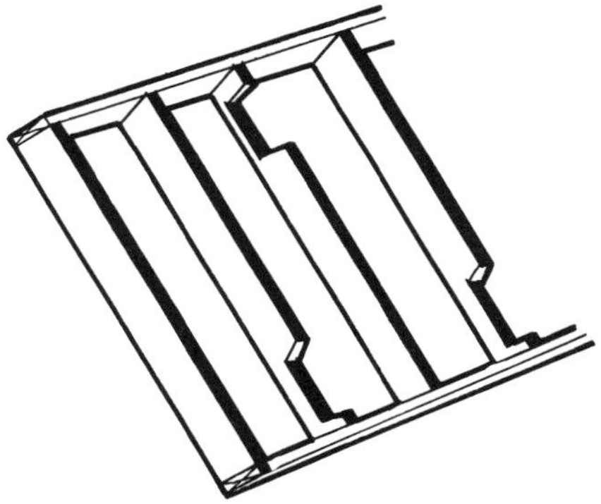

FIG. 9.15 COLLECTOR FRAMING

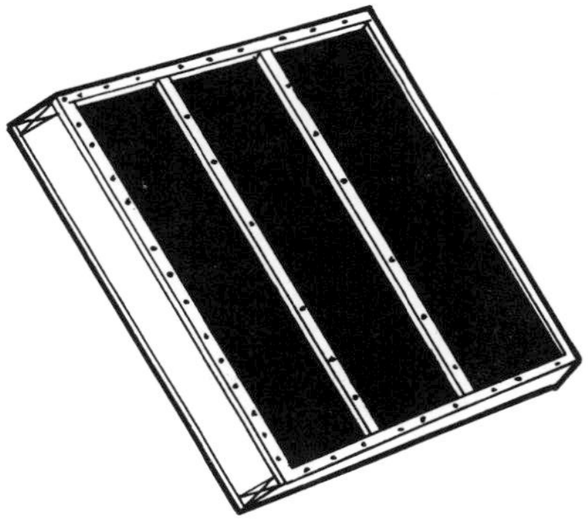

FIG. 9.16 FINAL PRODUCT

PHOTOVOLTAIC COLLECTOR

PHOTOVOLTAIC CELLS CONVERT SOLAR RADIATION INTO ELECTRICITY DIRECTLY. THE CONVERSION TAKES PLACE WHEN THE ELECTRONS IN ONE OF THE CRYSTAL LAYERS JUMP TO THE OTHER LAYER. THERE ARE TWO BASIC TYPES OF PHOTOVOLTAIC CELLS; THEY ARE THE SILICON CELL AND THE CADMUIM CELL. THE SILICON CELL HAS HIGHER EFFICIENCY, GREAT- ER DURABILITY AND THEREFORE HIGHER COST. WITH THE CONVERSION OF RADIATION INTO ELECTRICITY THERE ARISES A NEED FOR COOLING. SINCE PHOTO- VOLTAIC CELLS ARE ELECTRIC IN NATURE, IT IS NECESSARY TO USE A COOLANT NOT CONDUCTIVE IN NATURE.

THE POWER DERIVED FROM THE CELLS IS IN THE FORM OF DIRECT CURRENT (D.C.).

FIG. 9.18 ILLUSTRATES THE POWER DEMANDS DURING THE COURSE OF A DAY FOR A SINGLE FAMILY HOME (I), AND THE RELATIVE INTENSITY AND TIME OF DAY DURING WHICH POWER CAN BE PRODUCED WITH THE CELLS.

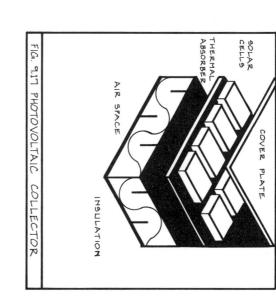

FIG. 9.17 PHOTOVOLTAIC COLLECTOR

SOLAR CELLS

THERMAL ABSORBER

COVER PLATE

AIR SPACE

INSULATION

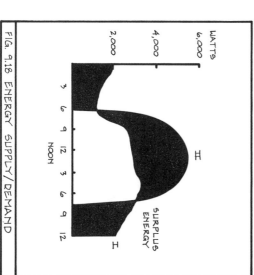

FIG. 9.18 ENERGY SUPPLY/DEMAND

WATTS

6,000

4,000

2,000

3 6 9 12 NOON 3 6 9 12

I

II

SURPLUS ENERGY

IN ORDER FOR CONCEN-
TRATING COLLECTORS TO
OPERATE EFFICIENTLY,
THEY MUST RECEIVE
DIRECT SOLAR RADIA-
TION. THEREFORE, THEY
SHOULD ONLY BE USED
IN AREAS WHERE THIS
CLIMATIC CHARACTERIS-
TIC IS PREVALENT.

FIGS. 9.19 AND 9.20
COMPARE THE CROSS-
SECTIONAL CONSTRUC-
TION OF A FLAT-PLATE
TO A CONCENTRATING
COLLECTOR.

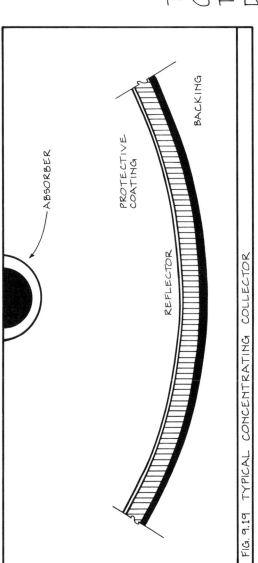

ABSORBER

PROTECTIVE
COATING

BACKING

REFLECTOR

FIG. 9.19 TYPICAL CONCENTRATING COLLECTOR

PROTECTIVE COVERS

CONDUCTING TUBES

HEAT ABSORBER

INSULATION

MANIFOLD

MANIFOLD

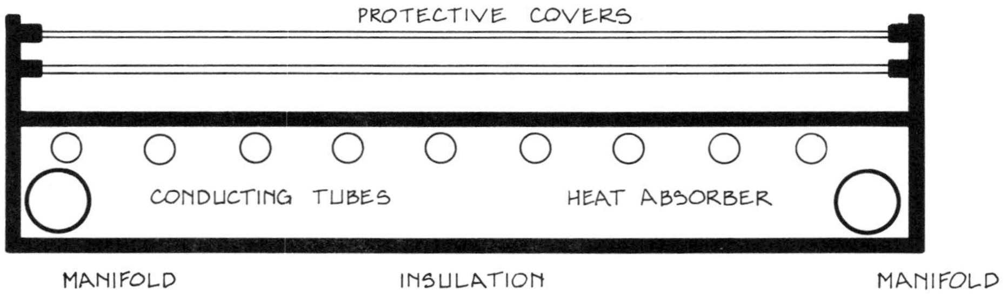

FIG. 9.20 TYPICAL FLAT-PLATE COLLECTOR

CONCENTRATING COLLECTOR

THE CHART LISTS SOME OF THE MAIN ADVANTAGES AND DISADVANTAGES OF THE CONCENTRATING COLLECTOR.

ADVANTAGES
1. AT A SET AMBIENT TEMPERATURE A CONCENTRATING COLLECTOR YIELDS HIGHER HEAT CONCENTRATIONS.
2. THEY HAVE HIGHER COLLECTION EFFICIENCY.
3. ENERGY STORAGE PER UNIT VOLUME IS GREATER.
4. CONCENTRATING COLLECTORS CAN BE USED TO GENERATE ELECTRICITY.

DISADVANTAGES
1. CONCENTRATING COLLECTORS GATHER MINIMUM AMOUNTS OF DIFFUSE RADIATION.
2. REFLECTANCE OF THE MIRROR MAY DECREASE WITH TIME.
3. ENERGY MUST BE USED TO TRACK THE SUN.
4. MAINTENANCE OF SYSTEM IS MORE INVOLVED.

THE STATIONARY RE-
FLECTOR TRACKING AB-
SORBER (SRTA) WAS IN-
VENTED BY W.G. STEW-
ARD. THE COLLECTOR
OPERATES ON THE PRIN-
CIPLE THAT REGARDLESS
OF THE SUN'S POSITION,
A SPHERICAL MIRROR
CAN FOCUS THE MAJOR-
ITY OF THE INCOMING
RADIATION ON A LINE
PARALLEL TO THE SUN'S
RAYS.

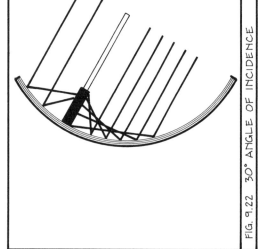

FIG. 9.22 30° ANGLE OF INCIDENCE

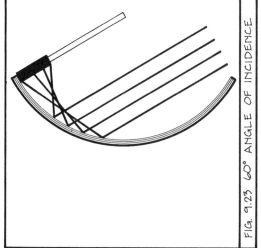

FIG. 9.23 60° ANGLE OF INCIDENCE

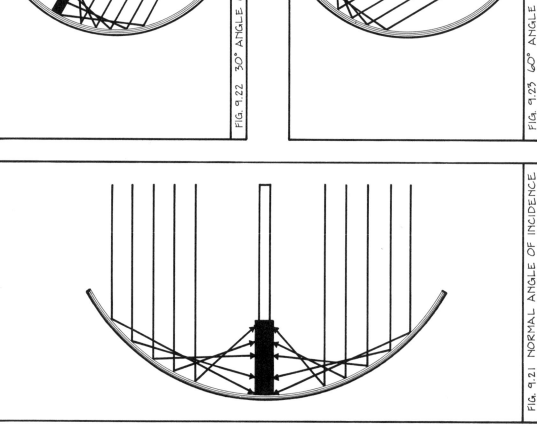

FIG. 9.21 NORMAL ANGLE OF INCIDENCE

FRESNEL-TYPE COLLECTOR

ONE OF THE DIFFICUL-
TIES INVOLVED IN THE USE
OF PARABOLIC COLLEC-
TORS IS THE SIZE AND
DEPTH THEY REQUIRE.
THE FRESNEL CONCEPT
OF SEGMENTING AND
COMPRESSING THE REFLEC-
TOR REDUCES THE INCON-
VENIENCE IN EXCHANGE
FOR A MINOR DROP IN
EFFICIENCY.

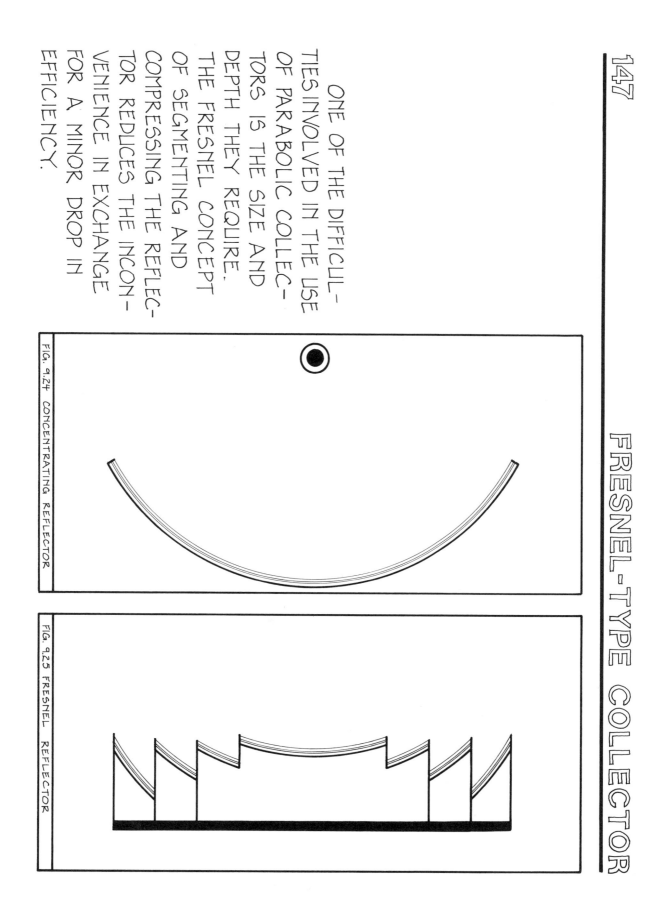

FIG. 9.24 CONCENTRATING REFLECTOR

FIG. 9.25 FRESNEL REFLECTOR

THE COMPOUND-PARA-
BOLIC-CONCENTRATOR,
(CPC), IS A NON-TRACK-
ING COLLECTOR. FIG. 9.26
ILLUSTRATES ITS CROSS
SECTION.

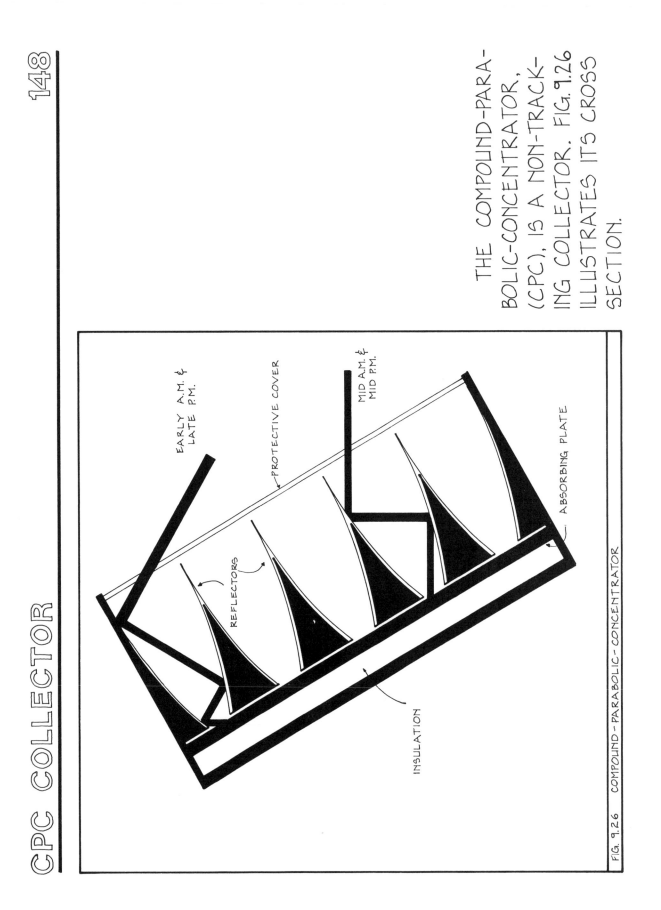

EARLY A.M. &
LATE P.M.

PROTECTIVE COVER

MID A.M. &
MID P.M.

REFLECTORS

ABSORBING PLATE

INSULATION

FIG. 9.26   COMPOUND-PARABOLIC-CONCENTRATOR

THE PYRAMIDAL-OPTIC
CONCENTRATOR IS PAT-
ENTED BY E.M. WORMSER.
THE CONCENTRATOR RE-
DUCES THE SIZE REQUIRE-
MENTS OF THE FLAT-
PLATE COLLECTOR BY A
FACTOR OF 2 TO 6. IN
ADDITION, AESTHETIC IN-
TEGRATION OF THE COL-
LECTOR AND BUILDING IS
FACILITATED DUE TO THE
COLLECTOR'S PROTEC-
TIVE ENCLOSURE.

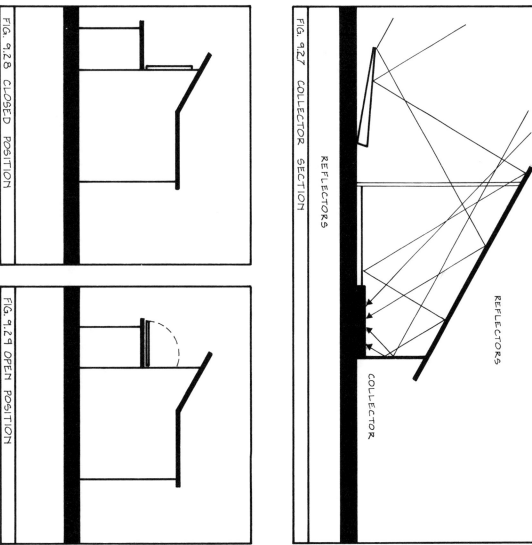

FIG. 9.27 COLLECTOR SECTION

REFLECTORS

REFLECTORS

COLLECTOR

FIG. 9.28 CLOSED POSITION

FIG. 9.29 OPEN POSITION

SOLAR HEAT CAN BE STORED IN TWO WAYS;
SENSIBLE HEAT STORAGE AND LATENT HEAT STORA-
AGE. SENSIBLE HEAT CAN BE STORED BY RAISING
THE TEMPERATURE OF SUCH MATERIALS AS ROCK,
WATER, ADOBE AND OTHERS. LATENT HEAT IS
STORED THROUGH THE FUSION OR EVAPORATION
ASSOCIATED WITH A MATERIAL WHEN THERE IS A
CHANGE OF STATE. THE FOLLOWING PAGES PRESENT
METHODS FOR STORING HEAT AS OPPOSED TO HEAT
STORAGE DEVICES.

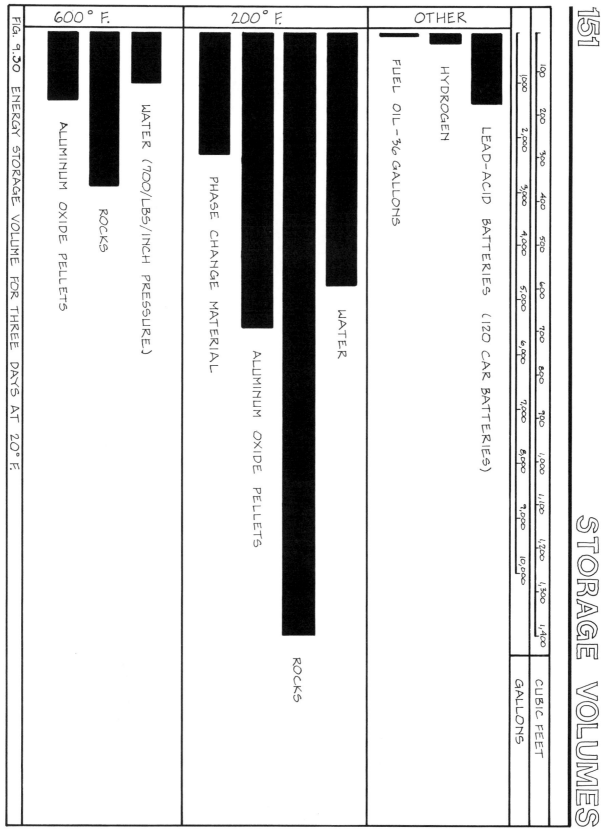

STORAGE VOLUMES

| | CUBIC FEET | GALLONS |

100 · 200 · 300 · 400 · 500 · 600 · 700 · 800 · 900 · 1,000 · 1,100 · 1,200 · 1,300 · 1,400

1,000 · 2,000 · 3,000 · 4,000 · 5,000 · 6,000 · 7,000 · 8,000 · 9,000 · 10,000

OTHER

LEAD-ACID BATTERIES (120 CAR BATTERIES)

HYDROGEN

FUEL OIL ~ 36 GALLONS

200° F.

WATER

ALUMINUM OXIDE PELLETS

ROCKS

PHASE CHANGE MATERIAL

600° F.

ALUMINUM OXIDE PELLETS

ROCKS

WATER (700/LBS/INCH PRESSURE)

FIG. 9.30 ENERGY STORAGE VOLUME FOR THREE DAYS AT 20° F.

ROCK STORAGE REQUIRES 2 TO 2½ TIMES MORE VOLUME THAN WATER STORAGE, ASSUMING EQUAL TEMPERATURE RANGE.

THE RECOMMENDED ROCK SIZE FOR HEAT STORAGE IS 2 INCHES IN DIAMETER. SMALLER ROCKS WILL INCREASE RESISTIVITY TO AIR FLOW. LARGER ROCKS WILL LEAVE TOO BIG A GAP BETWEEN THE ROCKS WHICH WILL INCREASE THE STORAGE VOLUME RE-QUIREMENTS.

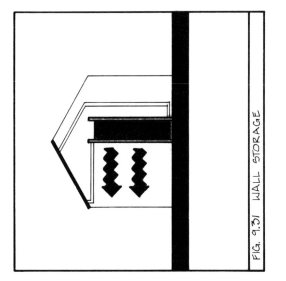

FIG. 9.31 WALL STORAGE

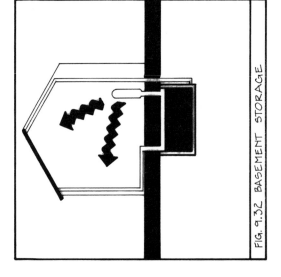

FIG. 9.32 BASEMENT STORAGE

WATER HAS THE HIGHEST CAPACITY TO RETAIN HEAT PER POUND THAN ANY OTHER READILY AVAILABLE MATERIAL. THE STORAGE TANK USED SHOULD BE PARTITIONED OFF OR ELSE SEVERAL TANKS SHOULD BE USED. THIS WILL ALLOW FOR CONTROLLED TEMPERATURE GRADATION.

FIG. 9.33 VERTICAL DRUM WALL

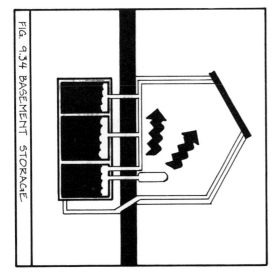

FIG. 9.34 BASEMENT STORAGE

NATURAL RADIATION IS THE HEAT FLOW
THROUGH ELECTROMAGNETIC WAVES WITHOUT
THE AID OF MECHANICAL ELEMENTS.

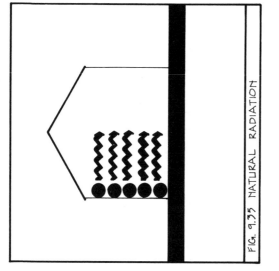

FIG. 9.35 NATURAL RADIATION

NATURAL CONVECTION IS THE AIR FLOW PRO-
DUCED THROUGH TEMPERATURE VARIATIONS WITH-
OUT THE AID OF MECHANICAL ELEMENTS.

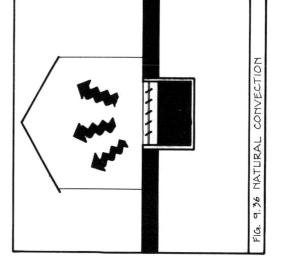

FIG. 9.36 NATURAL CONVECTION

FORCED AIR SYSTEMS USE MECHANICAL ELE-
MENTS TO PRODUCE THE REQUIRED AIR FLOW.
FORCED RADIATION RELIES ON THE TRANSFER
OF HEAT FROM CONTAINED WATER TO THE LIVING
SPACE.

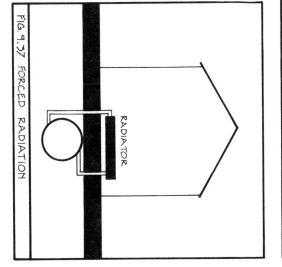

FIG. 9.37 FORCED RADIATION

RADIATOR

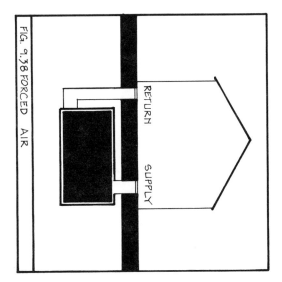

FIG. 9.38 FORCED AIR

RETURN   SUPPLY

APPENDIX A

SUNPATH DIAGRAMS

28°N LATITUDE

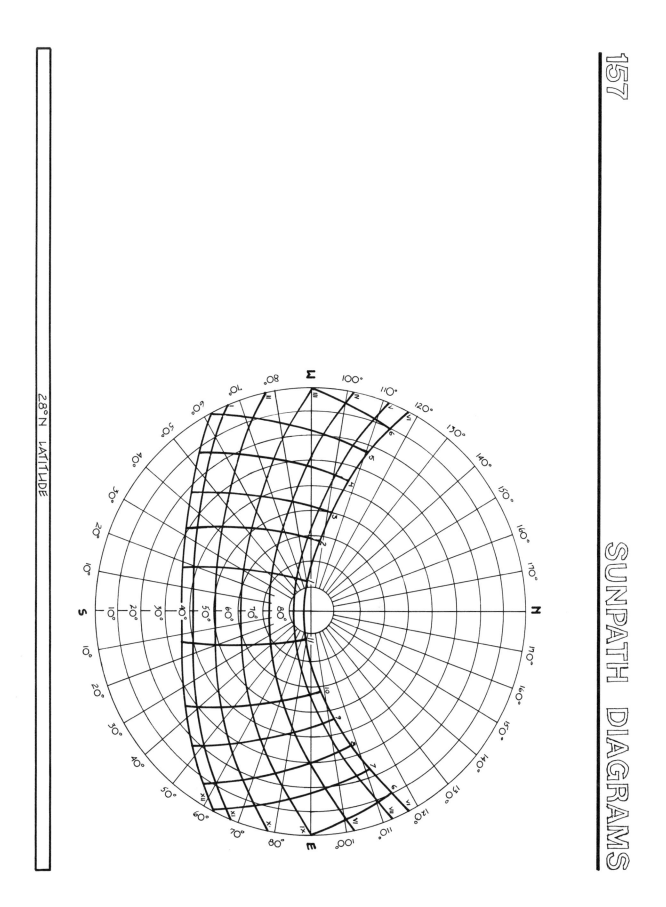

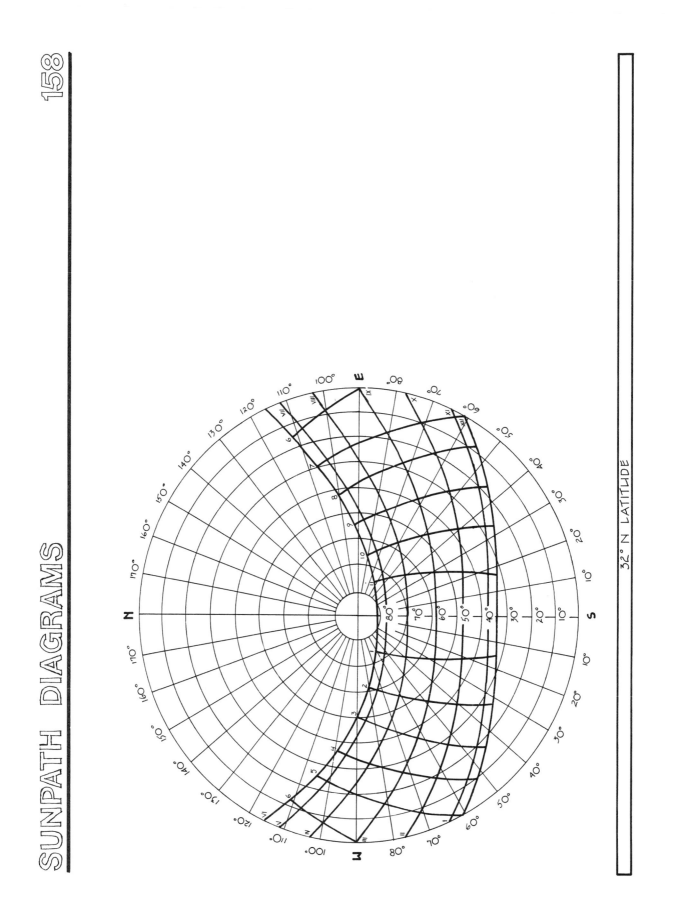

32° N LATITUDE

SUNPATH DIAGRAMS

36° N LATITUDE

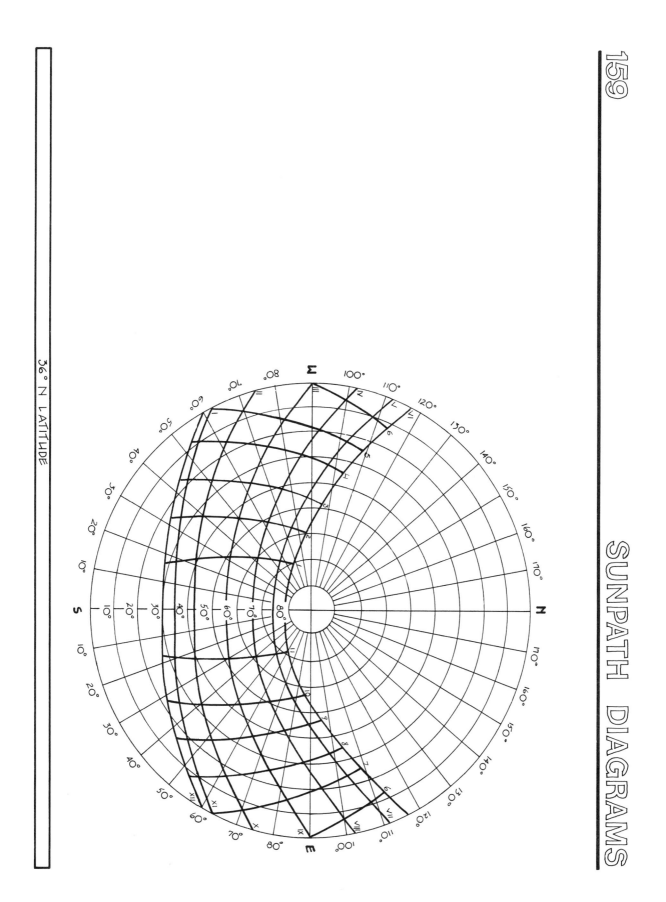

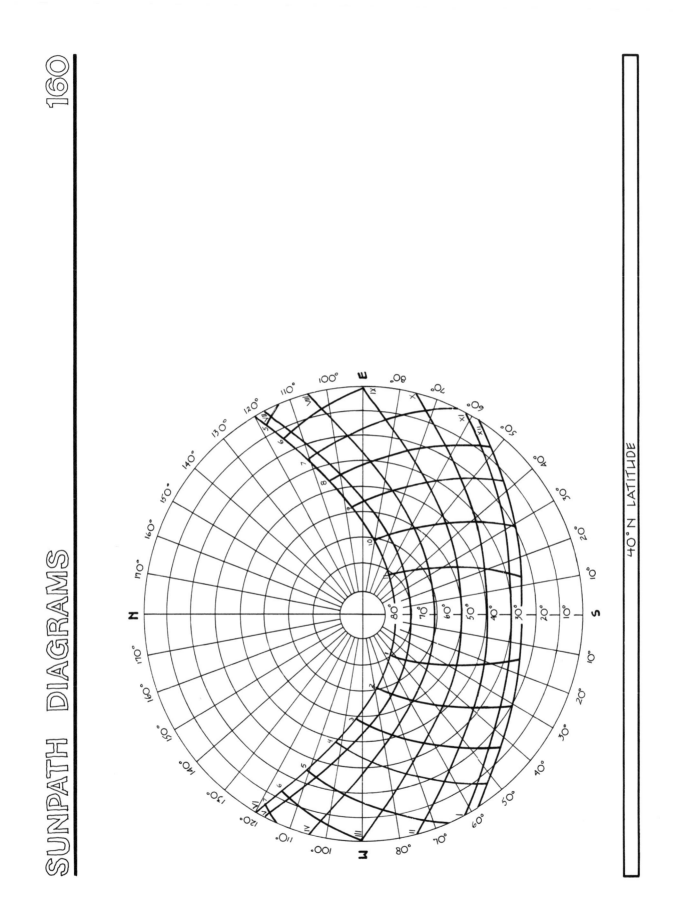

40°N LATITUDE

SUNPATH DIAGRAMS

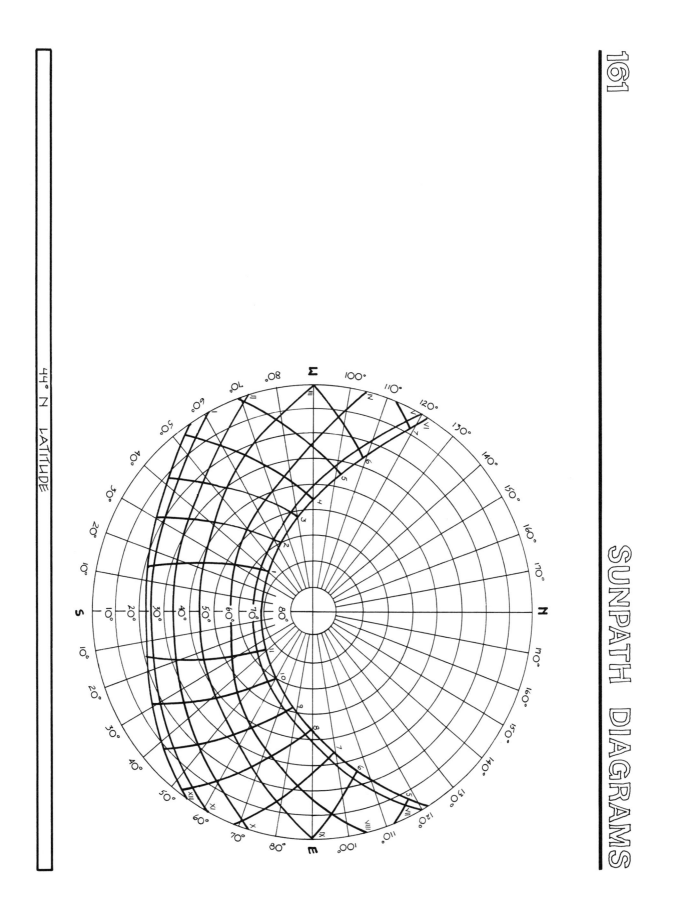

44° N LATITUDE

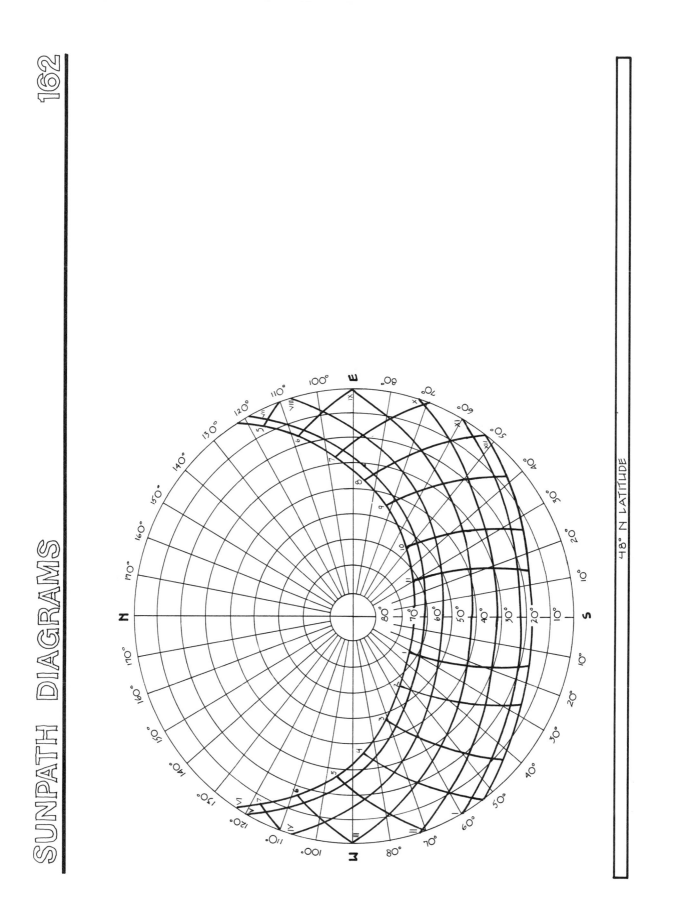

48° N LATITUDE

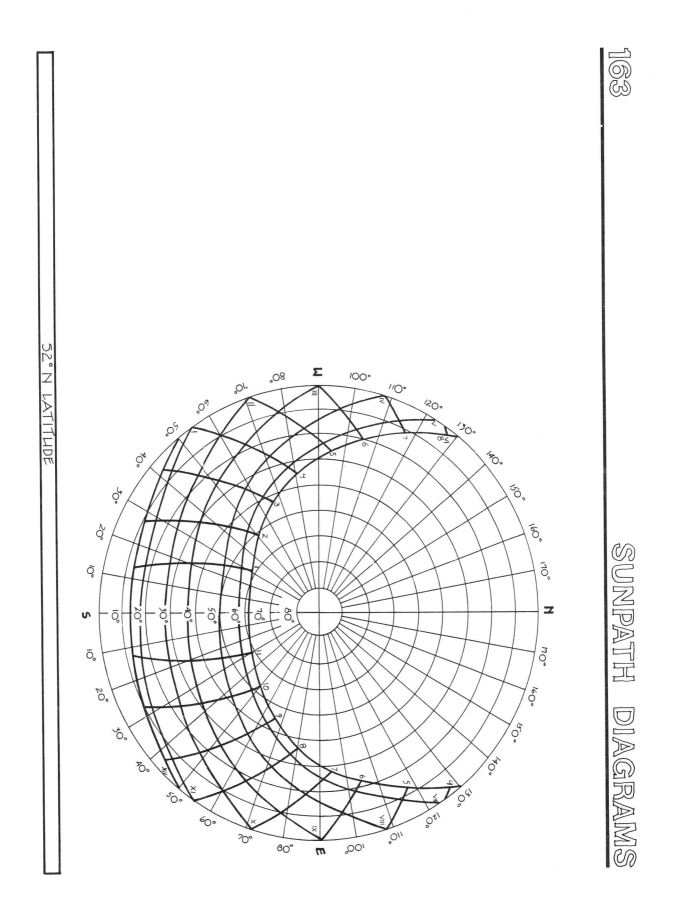

SUNPATH DIAGRAMS

52° N LATITUDE

ALTITUDE AND AZIMUTH OF THE SUN

$M = 0°.985600\ T + M_o$

$L = M + 1°.917\ SIN-M + 0°.020\ SIN\ 2M + L_o$

$TAN-\alpha = 0.91744\ TAN-L$

$SIN-\delta = 0.39787\ SIN-L$

$S = S_o + 360°.98547\ T - \lambda$

$H = S - \alpha$

$SIN-A = COZ-Z = SIN\ \phi\ SIN\delta + COS\ \phi\ COS\ \delta\ COS-H$

$TAN-X = \dfrac{-SIN-H}{COS\ \phi\ TAN\delta - SIN\ \phi\ COS-H}$

$A = 360° + X$ IF DENOMINATOR OF (H) IS POSITIVE AND H IS POSITIVE

$ = X$ IF DENOMINATOR OF (H) IS POSITIVE AND H IS NEGATIVE

$ = 180 + X$ IF DENOMINATOR OF (H) IS NEGATIVE

SUNPATH DIAGRAMS

WHERE:

t = NO. OF DAYS (PLUS FRACTION) ELAPSED SINCE JAN. 0, 0^H U.T.

M = MEAN ANOMALY OF SUN.

M_0 = MEAN ANOMALY OF SUN AT JAN. 0, 0^H U.T (SEE TABLE ON NEXT PAGE).

L = TRUE LONGITUDE OF SUN.

L_0 = LONGITUDE OF PERIGEE OF SUN (SEE TABLE ON NEXT PAGE).

α = RIGHT ASCENSION OF SUN.

δ = DECLINATION OF SUN.

λ = OBSERVER'S LONGITUDE (WEST IS POSITIVE, EAST IS NEGATIVE).

ϕ = OBSERVER'S LATITUDE (NORTH IS POSITIVE, SOUTH IS NEGATIVE).

S = SIDEREAL TIME.

S_0 = SIDEREAL TIME AT GREENWICH AT JAN. 0, 0^H U.T (SEE TABLE ON NEXT PG.).

h = HOUR ANGLE OF SUN.

a = ALTITUDE OF SUN.

z = ZENITH DISTANCE OF SUN = 90° − a.

X = AZIMUTH ANGLE.

A = TRUE AZIMUTH OF SUN.

TABLE OF M_o, L_o, S_o.

YEAR	M_o	L_o	S_o
1976	-3.71982	282.°53116	98.°79712
1977	-2.99009	282.54836	99.54405
1978	-3.24595	282.56550	99.30533
1979	-3.50182	282.58265	99.06662

THE ABOVE FORMULAS, EVALUATED IN THE ORDER GIVEN, ALLOW THE COMPUTATION OF THE ALTITUDE (a) AND THE TRUE AZIMUTH (A) OF THE SUN FOR SOME TIME "t" AT A LOCATION ON THE EARTH AT LONGITUDE "λ" AND LATITUDE "ϕ". QUANTITIES NEEDED IN EACH FORMULA ARE COMPUTED FROM THE PRECEEDING EXPRESSIONS. NOTE THAT ALL ANGULAR QUANTITIES (INCLUDING THE SIDEREAL TIME "S") ARE EXPRESSED IN DEGREES.

THE TIME "T" OF THE OBSERVATION MUST BE EXPRESSED IN "UNIVERSAL TIME" (UT)=GREENWICH MEAN TIME (GMT); SPECIFICALLY, IT MUST BE THE NO. OF DAYS (PLUS FRACTION) ELAPSED TIME 0^h UT OF JANUARY 0 (= 0^h UT DEC. 31 OF PRECEDING YEAR). FOR EXAMPLE, THE TIME 3:43 P.M. EST ON MARCH 11, 1977 IS "T" = 70.863194.

IN FORMULA (A), USE THE VALUE OF M. GIVEN IN THE TABLE FOR THE YEAR.   IN FORMULA (B), USE THE VALUE OF L, GIVEN IN THE TABLE FOR THE YEAR.   IN FORMULA (C), THE CORRECT QUADRANT OF "a" MUST BE OBTAIN- ED; "a" IS IN THE SAME QUADRANT AS "L".   IN FORMULA (E), "S" SHOULD BE REDUCED TO A VALUE BETWEEN -180° AND +180°.

NOTE THAT FORMULAS (G) AND (H) ARE IDENTICAL TO FORMULAS (2) AND (3) IN USNO CIRCULAR NO. 138.

APPENDIX B

MEAN SOLAR RADIATION

FEBRUARY

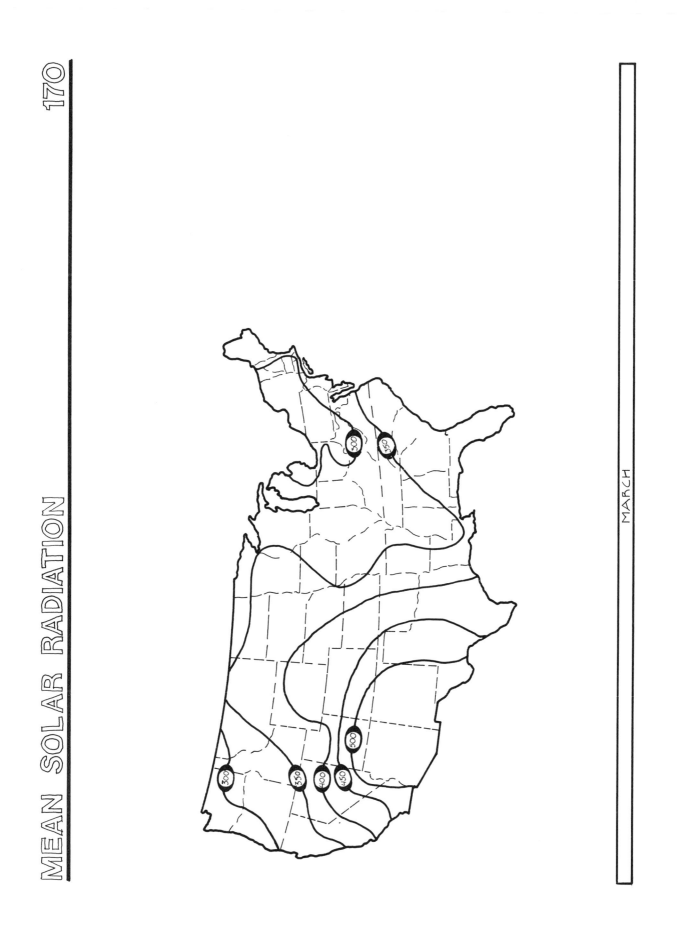

MARCH

APRIL

MEAN SOLAR RADIATION

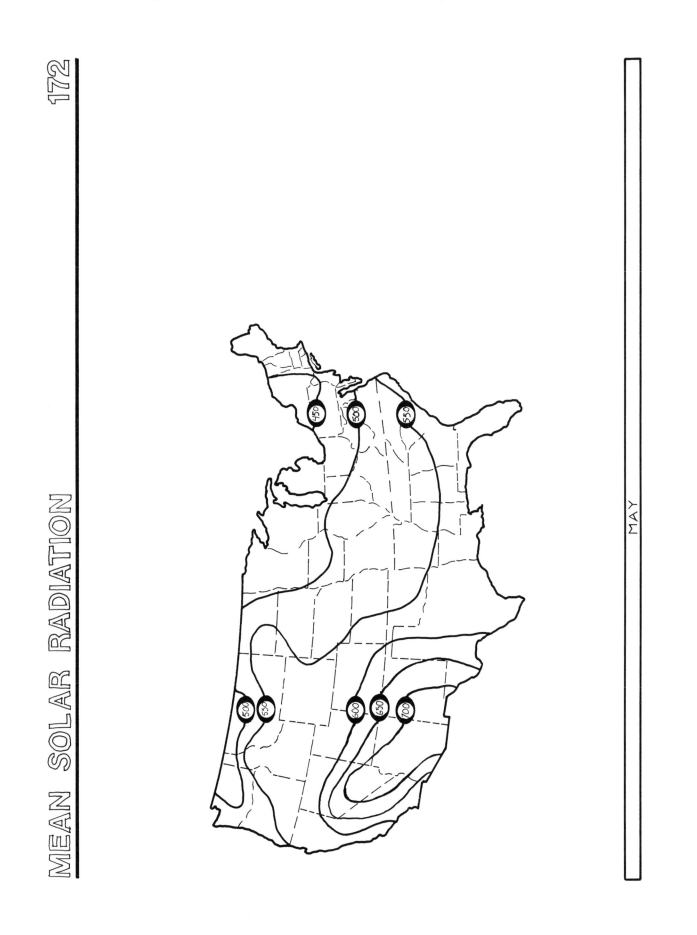

MAY

MEAN SOLAR RADIATION

JUNE

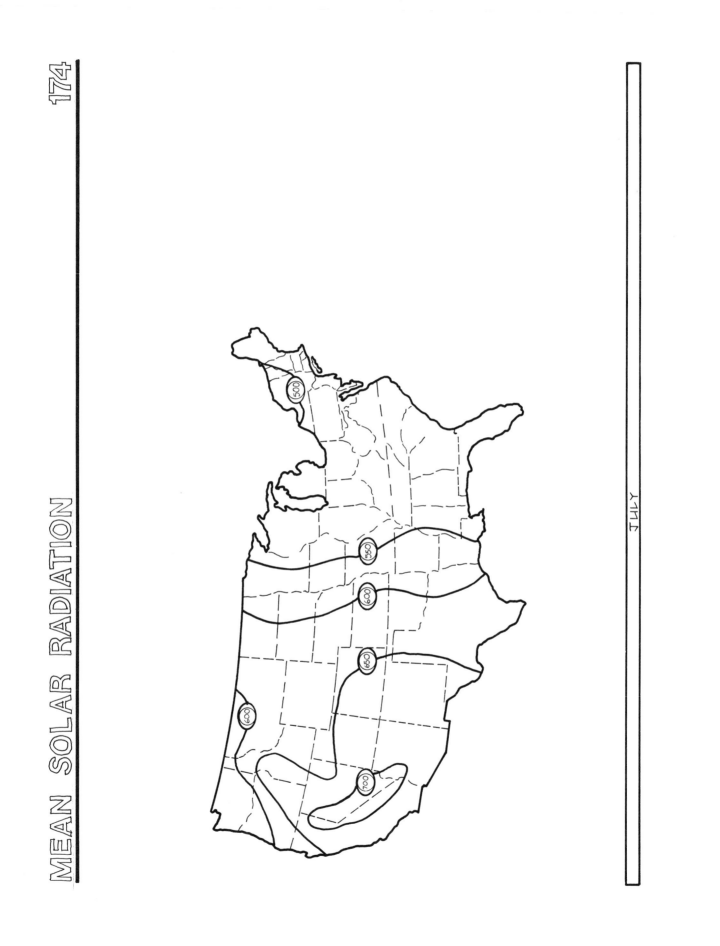

JULY

MEAN SOLAR RADIATION

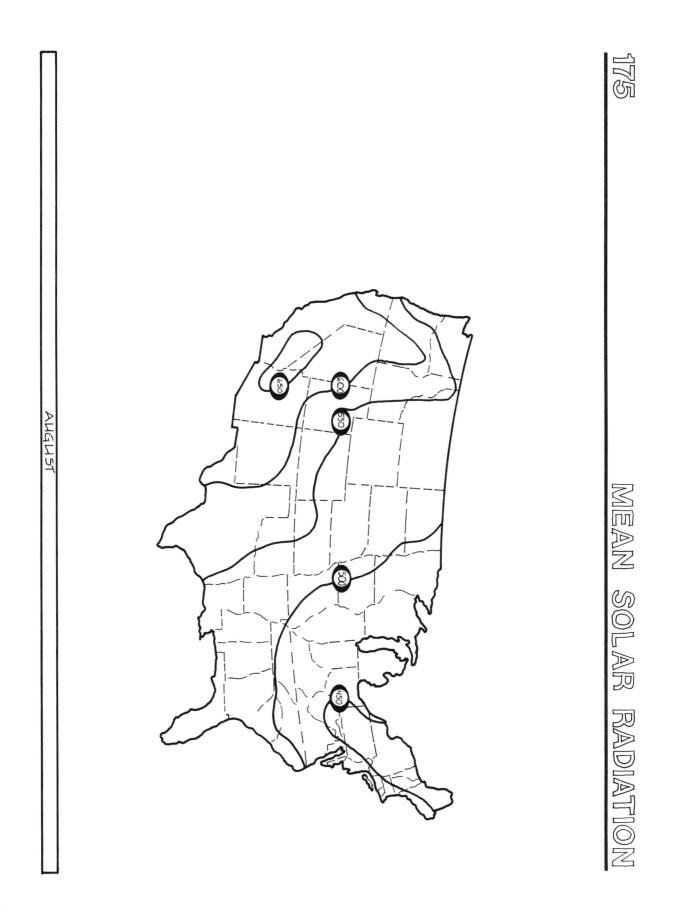

AUGUST

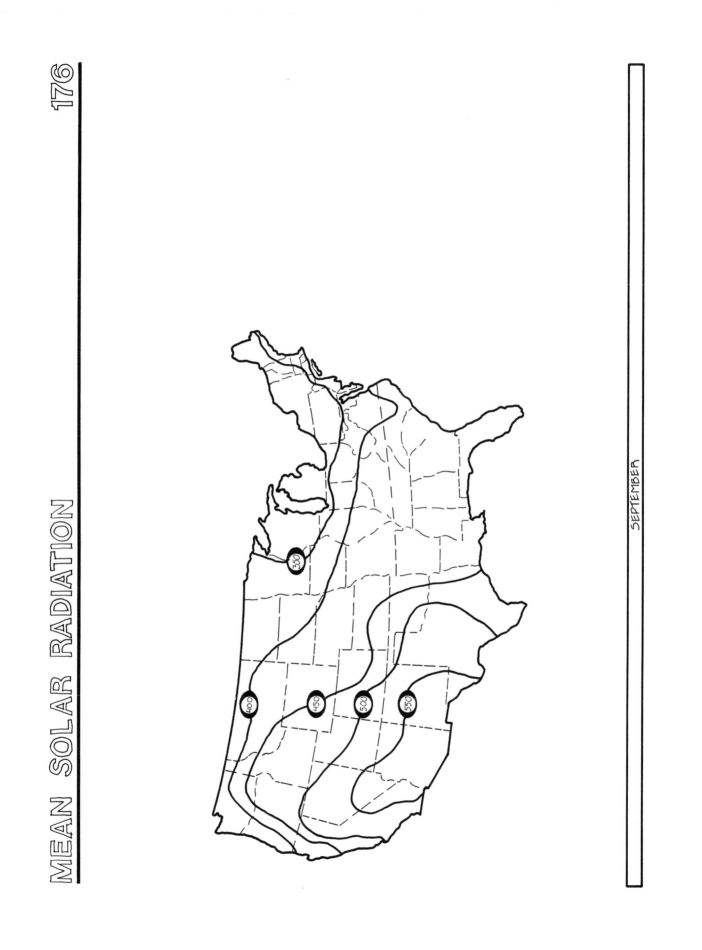

SEPTEMBER

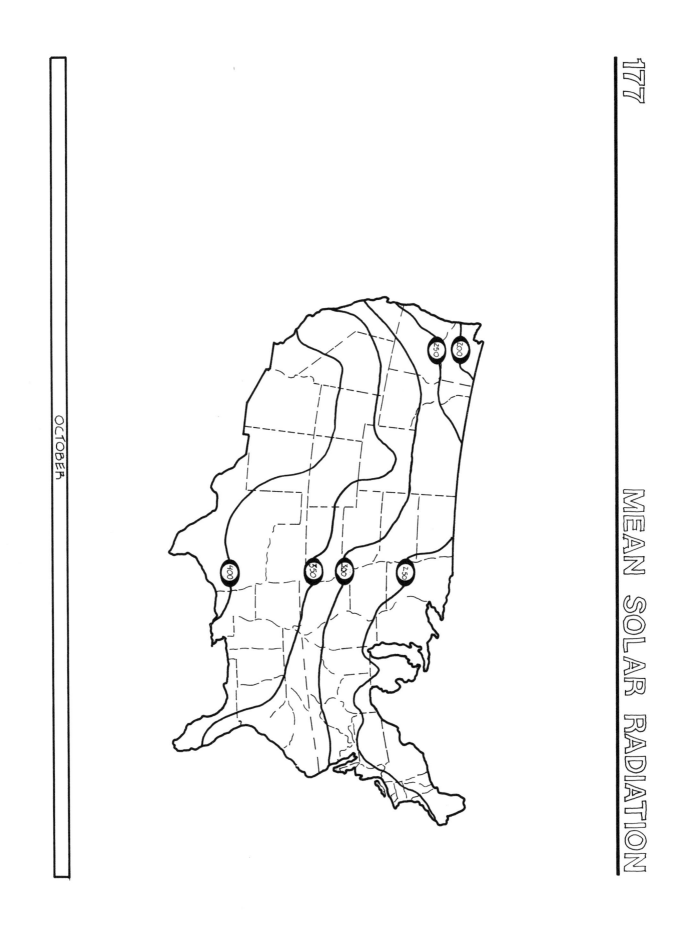

MEAN SOLAR RADIATION

OCTOBER

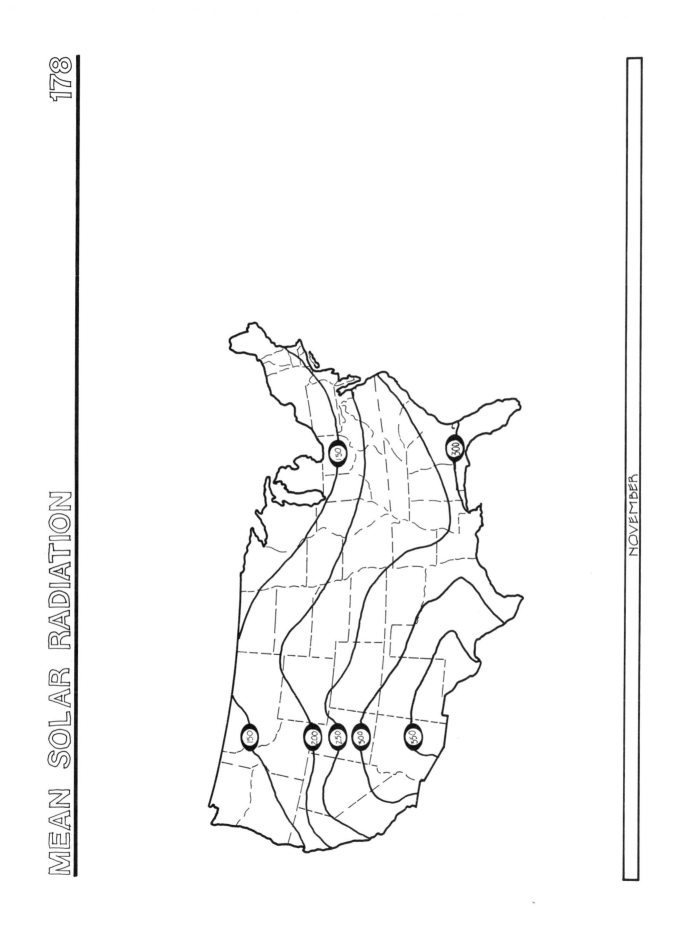

NOVEMBER

MEAN SOLAR RADIATION

DECEMBER

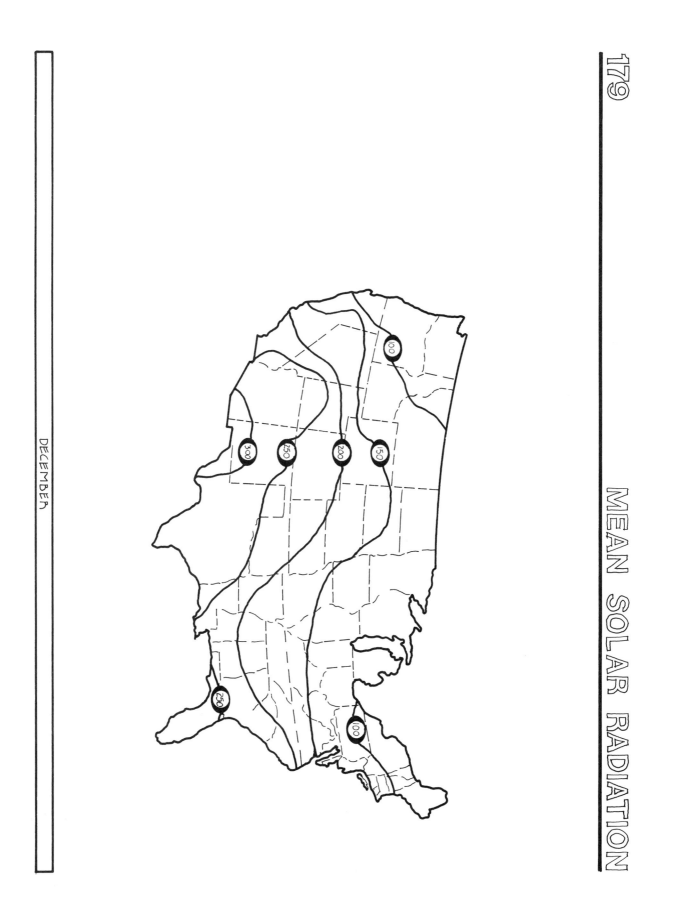

APPENDIX C

CONVERSION FACTORS

THERMAL CONDUCTIVITY

BTU/HR/FT/°F	1.731	W/M/°K
W/M/°K	0.5779	BTU/HR/FT/°F
W/CM/°C	57.79	BTU/HR/FT/°F
CAL/MIN/CM/°C	14,514	BTU/HR/FT/°F
CAL/SEC/CM/°C	241.9	BTU/HR/FT/°F

TEMPERATURE

°R	−459.7	°F
°C	+273.1	°K
°K	−273.1	°C
°F	=5/9(°F−32)	°C
°C	=9/5(°C+32)	°F
°F	+459.7	°R

CONVERSION FACTORS

HEAT FLUX

FT. LB.	13.272	BTU/HR./FT².
W/CM²	3171	BTU/HR/FT²
BTU/HR./SQ FT.	3.154×10^{-4}	W/CM²
BTU/HR/SQ FT.	3.154	W/M²
LANGLEY (LY)	3.687	BTU/FT².
LY/MIN.	221.2	BTU/HR/FT²
BTU/HR.	0.293	WATT
WATT	3.414	BTU/HR.
TON AIR CONDITIONING	12,000	BTU/HR.

HEAT TRANSFER COEFFICIENT

BTU/HR/FT²/F	5.67	W/M²/°K
W/M²/°K	0.1761	BTU/HR./FT²/°F.
W/CM²/°C	1.761	BTU/HR./FT²/°F.
CAL/HR./CM²/°C	2.048	BTU/HR/FT²/°F

CONVERSION FACTORS

LENGTH

IN.	0.0833	FT.
FT.	12.0	IN.
IN.	2.54	CM.
CM.	0.394	IN.
METER	39.37	IN.
μ	3.937×10^{-5}	IN.
IN	2.54×10^{4}	μ

MASS

LB.	454	G
LB.	0.454	KILOGRAM
K.G.	2.205	LB.

ENERGY AND POWER

FT.LB.	1.29×10^{-3}	BTU.
BTU.	778	FT.LB.
K-CAL.	3.968	BTU.
CAL.	4.186	JOULE
JOULE	9.478×10^{-4}	BTU
BTU.	1055.1	JOULE
KW-HR.	3413	BTU.
BTU.	2.93×10^{-4}	KW-HR.
H.P.	2544	BTU/HR.
H.P.	745.7	WATT(W)

APPENDIX D

ALTEN ASSOCIATES
2594 LEGHORN ST.
MOUNTAIN VIEW, CA.

SYSTEMS   SPACE AND WATER
           HEATING

AMERICAN HELIOTHERMAL CO.
3515 TAMARAC DRIVE
DENVER, COLORADO

COLLECTOR   SPACE AND WATER
             HEATING

AMETEK
ONE SPRING AVE.
HATFIELD, PA.

COLLECTOR   SPACE COOLING

AMERICAN SOLAR POWER INC.
5018 W GRACE ST.
TAMPA. FLA.

SYSTEM   WATER HEATING

ARKLA INDUSTRIES
810 E, FRANKLIN ST.
EVANSVILLE, INDIANA

CHILLER   AIR CONDITIONING
ABSORPTION

BROWN MANUFACTURING CO.
P.O. BOX 14546
OKLAHOMA CITY, OKLA.

PARABOLIC   ALL USES
COLLECTOR

BORG-WARNER CORP.
P.O. BOX 1592
YORK, PA.

ABSORPTION
CHILLER

AIR CONDITIONING

BURKE RUBBER CO.
2250 S. 10TH ST.
SAN JOSE, CA.

SYSTEM

SWIMMING POOL HEATER

C. S. I.
12400 49TH ST
CLEARWATER FLA.

COLLECTOR

WATER AND
SPACE HEATING

C & C SOLARTHERMICS, INC.
BOX 144, RD. 3
SMITHSBURG, MD.

DETACHED
SYSTEM

SPACE HEATING

EL CAMINO SOLAR SYSTEMS
5511-C EKWILL ST.
SANTA BARBARA, CA.

SYSTEM

WATER HEATING

CHAMBERLAIN MANUFACTURING CO.
845 LARCH AVE.
ELMHURST, ILLINOIS

FLAT PLATE
COLLECTOR

WATER &
SPACE HEATING

CONTEMPORARY SYSTEMS
G8 CHARLONNE ST.
JAFFREY N.H.

SYSTEMS

SPACE AND WATER HEATING

DI-SOL, INC.
BOX G14
MARLBORO, MA.

SYSTEMS

SPACE AND WATER HEATING

GIER-DUNKLE INC.
1718 21ST ST.
SANTA MONICA, CAL.

CONTROL

ENERGY DYNAMICS CORP.
327 W. YERMIJO AVE.
COLORADO SPRINGS, COL.

COLLECTOR

SPACE AND WATER HEATING

ENVIRONMENTAL DESIGNS
BOX 12408
MEMPHIS, TENN

COLLECTOR

SPACE AND WATER HEATING

EDWARDS ENGINEERING
101 ALEXANDER AVE.
POMPTON PLAINS, N.J.

SYSTEMS

SPACE AND WATER HEATING

ENVIRONMENTAL ENERGIES, INC. COLLECTOR   SPACE AND WATER
FRONT ST. BOX 73   HEATING
COPEMISH, MICH.

FAFCO, INC.   COLLECTOR   SPACE AND WATER
138 JEFERSON DRIVE   HEATING
MENLO PARK, CAL.

FALBEL ENERGY SYSTEMS   PARABOLIC   SPACE AND WATER
472 WESTOVER ROAD   COLLECTOR   HEATING
STAMFORD, CONN.

FORD PRODUCTS CORPORA-   STORAGE   SPACE AND WATER
TION   TANK   HEATING
VALLEY COTTAGE, N.Y.

FUTURE SYSTEMS, INC.   SYSTEM   SPACE AND WATER
12500 WEST CEDAR DRIVE   HEATING
LAKEWOOD, COL.

GARDEN WAY LABS   COLLECTOR   SPACE AND WATER
CHARLOTTE,   HEATING
VERMONT

MANUFACTURERS OF SOLAR PRODUCTS

G.D.C.
3424 SOUTH STATE ST.
CHICAGO, ILL.

SYSTEMS   SPACE AND WATER HEATING

GENERAL ELECTRIC, INC.
KING OF PRUSSIA PARK
PHILADELPHIA, PENN.

SYSTEMS   SPACE AND WATER HEATING

GRUMMAN CORPORATION
BETH PAGE,
NEW YORK

SYSTEMS   SPACE AND WATER HEATING

GULF THERMAL CORP.
BOX 13124 AIR GATE DRIVE
SARASOTA, FLA.

COLLECTOR   SPACE AND WATER HEATING

HONEYWELL
2600 RIDGEWAY PARKWAY
MINNEAPOLIS, MINN.

CONTROLS   SPACE AND WATER HEATING

ILSE ENGINEERING
7177 ARROWHEAD ROAD
DULUTH, MINN.

COLLECTOR   SPACE AND WATER HEATING

INDEPENDENT LIVING INC.
5715 BUFORD HIGHWAY N.E.
DOROVILLE, GA.

SYSTEMS   SPACE AND WATER
HEATING

INTERNATIONAL ENVIRONMETAL CO.
129 HALSTEAD AVE.
MAMARONECK, N.Y.

SYSTEMS   SPACE AND WATER
HEATING

W.L. JACKSON MFG CO.
BOX 11168
CHATTANOOGA, TENN.

COLLECTOR &   SPACE AND WATER
STORAGE   HEATING

JOHNSON CONTROLS
2221 CAMDEN COURT
OAK BROOK, ILL.

CONTROLS

J.G. JOHNSTONS CO.
33458 ANGLES FORREST HGWY.
PALMDALE, CAL.

COLLECTOR   SPACE AND WATER
HEATING

K.T.A. CORPORATION
12300 WASHINGTON AVE.
ROCKVILLE, MD.

COLLECTOR   SPACE AND WATER
HEATING

MANUFACTURERS OF SOLAR PRODUCTS

KALWALL CORP.
88 PINE ST. BOX 237
MANCHESTER, N.H.   SYSTEMS   SPACE AND WATER HEATING

KENNECOTT COPPER CORP.
128 SPRING ST.
LEXINGTON, MASS.   COLLECTOR   SPACE AND WATER HEATING

L.O.F. SOLAR ENERGY SYS.
811 MADISON AVE.
TOLEDO, OHIO   COLLECTOR   SPACE AND WATER HEATING

MANKIND RESEARCH, UNLTD.
1640 KALMIA ROAD N.W.
WASHINGTON, D.C.   COLLECTOR   SPACE AND WATER HEATING

Mc ARTHURS, INC.
BOX 238
FOREST CITY, N.C.   COLLECTOR   SPACE AND WATER HEATING

NATIONAL SOLAR SUPPLY CO.
2331 ADAMS DRIVE, N.W.
ATLANTA, GA.   COLLECTOR   SPACE AND WATER HEATING

OLIN BRASS
EAST ALTON,
ILLINOIS

COLLECTOR SPACE AND WATER HEATING

OWENS-ILLINOIS
BOX 1035
TOLEDO, OHIO

COLLECTOR SPACE AND WATER HEATING

PIPER HYDRO, INC.
2875 EAST LA PALMA
ANAHEIM, CAL.

COLLECTOR SPACE AND WATER HEATING

P. P. G.
ONE GATEWAY CENTER
PITTSBURG, PA.

COLLECTOR SPACE AND WATER HEATING

R-M PRODUCTS
5010 COOK ST.
DENVER, COLO.

COLLECTOR SPACE AND WATER HEATING

RANCO
BOX 8187
COLUMBUS, OHIO

CONTROLS

MANUFACTURERS OF SOLAR PRODUCTS

REFRIGERATION RESEARCH 525 NORTH 5TH ST. BRIGHTON, MICH.	SYSTEM	SPACE AND WATER HEATING
REVERE COPPER & BRASS INC. BOX 151 ROME, N.Y.	COLLECTOR	SPACE AND WATER HEATING
REYNOLDS METALS INC. BOX 27003 RICHMOND, VA.	COLLECTOR	SPACE AND WATER HEATING
RHO SIGMA 15150 RAYMER ST. VAN NUYS, CAL.	CONTROLS	
RHEEM MANUFACTURING CO. 7600 S. KEDSIE AVE. CHICAGO, ILL.	STORAGE	WATER HEATING
ROBERTSHAW LONGBEACH, CAL.	CONTROLS	

S.S.P. ASSOCIATES   COLLECTOR   SPACE AND WATER
704 BLUEHILL RD.   HEATING
RIVER VALE, N.J.

SEMCO   COLLECTOR   SPACE AND WATER
1091 S W IST WAY   HEATING
DEERFIELD BEACH, FLA.

SENNERGETICS SOLAR PROD.   COLLECTOR   SPACE AND WATER
18621 PARTHENIA ST.   HEATING
NORTH RIDGE, CAL.

SENSOR TECHNOLOGY, INC.   PHOTOVOLTAIC   ELECTRICITY
21012 LASSEN ST.
CHATSWORTH, CAL.

SHELDAHL   CONCENTRATING   SPACE AND WATER
NORTH FIELD,   COLLECTOR   HEATING
MINN.

SKY-THERM   SYSTEM   SPACE HEATING
2424 WILSHIRE BLVD.
LOS ANGELES, CAL.

DEL-SOL CONTROL CORP.   CONTROL
11914 U.S.1
JUNO, FLA.

SOL AIRE   COLLECTOR   SPACE   AND   WATER
20948 CORSAIR BLVD.   HEATING
HAYWARD, CAL.

SOLAR APPLICATIONS, INC.   CONCENTRATING SPACE   AND   WATER
7426 CONVOY COURT   COLLECTOR   HEATING
SAN DIEGO, CAL.

SOLAR DEVELOPMENT INC.   COLLECTOR   SPACE   AND   WATER
4180 WESTROADS DR.   HEATING
WEST PALM BEACH, FLA.

SOLAR DYNAMICS, INC.   SYSTEM   SPACE   AND   WATER
4527 E. 11TH AVE.   HEATING
HIALEAH, FLA.

SOLAR ENERGY CO.   PHOTOVOLTAIC   ELECTRICITY
BOX 649
GLOUCESTER POINT, VA.

SOLAR ENERGY SYSTEMS, INC.   COLLECTOR   SPACE AND WATER HEATING
9016 COLLINS AVE.
PENNSAUKEN, N.J.

SOLAR ENGINEERING, INC.   COLLECTOR   SPACE AND WATER HEATING
BOX 3016, 110 PEACH ROAD
OAK RIDGE, TENN.

SOLERGY   CONCENTRATING COLLECTOR   SPACE AND WATER HEATING
70 ZOE ST.
SAN FRANCISCO, CAL.

SOLAR, INC.   COLLECTOR   SPACE AND WATER HEATING
BOX 246
MEAD, NEB.

SOLAR KING   SYSTEM   SPACE AND WATER HEATING
6801 NEW McGREGOR HGWY.
WACO, TX.

SOLAR MANUFACTURING CO.   SYSTEM   SPACE AND WATER HEATING
40 CONNEAUT LAKE RD.
GREENVILLE, PA.

SOLAR-PHYSICS, INC.
1350 "A" HILL ST.
EL CAJON, CAL.
    CONCENTRATING SPACE AND WATER
    COLLECTOR HEATING

SOLAR POWER CORP.
5 EXECUTIVE PARK DRIVE
NORTH BILLERICA, MASS.
    PHOTOVOLTAIC ELECTRICITY

SOLAR SENSOR SYSTEM
4220 BERRITT ST.
FAIRFAX, VA.
    CONTROL

SOLAR SERVICES, INC.
BOX 2166
HENDERSONVILLE, N.C.
    COLLECTOR SPACE AND WATER
    HEATING

SOLAR TECHNOLOGY CORP.
2160 CLAY ST.
DENVER, COL.
    SOLAR SPACE HEATING
    GARDEN

SOLAR SYSTEMS, INC.
1500 DURAND AVE.
RACINE, WISC.
    COLLECTOR SPACE AND WATER
    HEATING

MANUFACTURERS OF SOLAR PRODUCTS

SOLAR-THERMICS ENTERPRISES, LTD. SYSTEM   SPACE AND WATER HEATING
BOX 248
CRESTON, IOWA

SALARAY, INC.   COLLECTOR   SPACE AND WATER HEATING
324 S. KIDDE ST.
WHITEWATER, WISC.

SOLARON CORP.   SYSTEM   SPACE AND WATER HEATING
4850 OLIVES ST.
COMMERCE CITY, COLO.

SUN WALL, INC.   COLLECTOR   SPACE AND WATER HEATING
BOX 9723
PITTSBURGH, PA.

SOLUS, INC.   COLLECTOR & CONTROL   SPACE AND WATER HEATING
BOX 35227
HOUSTON, TX.

SOLOREX CORP.   PHOTOVOLTAIC ELECTRICITY
1335 PICCARD DR.
ROCKVILLE, MD.

MANUFACTURERS OF SOLAR PRODUCTS

ST. INDUSTRIES, INC.
ASHLAND CITY,
TENNESSEE

SYSTEM   WATER HEATING

MR. SUN, INC.
501 ARCHDALE DR.
CHARLOTTE, N.C.

SYSTEM   WATER HEATING

SUN POWER SYSTEMS
1121 LEWIS AVE.
SARASOTA, FLA.

PHOTOVOLTAIC ELECTRICITY

SUN SAVER, INC.
1611 9TH STREET
WHITE BEAR LAKE, MINN.

SYSTEM   SPACE AND WATER
HEATING

SUNSHINE SOLAR ENERGY EQ.
BOX 941
SHEBOYGAN, WISC.

SYSTEM   SPACE AND WATER
HEATING

SUNEARTH, INC.
RD. 1 BOX 337
GREEN LAKE, PA.

COLLECTOR   SPACE AND WATER
HEATING

SUN WORKS, INC.
669 BOSTON POST ROAD
GUILFORD, CONN.

SYSTEM   SPACE AND WATER
          HEATING

SWEDCAST CORP.
7350 EMPIRE DR.
FLORENCE, KEN.

COLLECTOR   SPACE AND WATER
             HEATING

THOMASON SOLAR HOMES, INC.
6802 WALKER MILL ROAD.
WASHINGTON, D.C.

SYSTEM   SPACE AND WATER
          HEATING

TRANTER, INC.
735 EAST HAZEL ST.
LANSING, MICH.

COLLECTOR   SPACE AND WATER
             HEATING

TROLA-TEMP
740 FEDERAL AVE.
KENILWORTH, N.J.

DISTRIBUTION &
CONTROLS

UNIT ELECTRIC CONTROL, INC.
130 ATLANTIC DR.
MAITLAND, FLA.

SYSTEM   WATER HEATING

	CONTROLS	SYSTEM SPACE AND WATER HEATING	SYSTEM WATER HEATING

VERTEX CORP.
808 106TH N.E.
BELLEVUE, WA.

WESTINGHOUSE ELECTRIC, CO.   SYSTEM SPACE AND WATER
BALTIMORE,   HEATING
MARYLAND

THE WILCON CORP.   SYSTEM WATER HEATING
3310 S.W. 7TH
OCALA, FLA.

APPENDIX E

BIBLIOGRAPHY AND SOURCES

1. SOLAR CONTROL AND SHADING DEVICES, VICTOR OLGAY A.I.A. ASSOCIATE PROFESSOR, PRINCETON UNIVERSITY

2-3. IBID

4. U.S. CLIMATIC ATLAS

5-14. IBID

15. U.S. WATER ATLAS

16.17. U.S. CLIMATIC ATLAS

18. THERMAL COMFORTS, EGAN

19-25. IBID

26. LOW-COST ENERGY EFFICIENT SHELTER FOR OWNERS AND BUILDERS, E. ECCLI

27-29. IBID

30. OBSERVATIONS ON THE FORGOTTEN ART OF BUILDING A GOOD FIREPLACE, VREST ORTON

NON-TECHNICAL

THE BUY WISE GUIDE TO SOLAR HEAT - F. HICKOK; HOUR HOUSE, P.O. BOX 40082, ST. PETERSBURG, FLA. 33743, 1976

DIRECT USE OF THE SUN'S ENERGY - F DANIELS; BALLANTINE BOOKS, INC., WESTMINSTER, MD. 21157, 1964

BIBLIOGRAPHY AND SOURCES

YOUR HOME'S SOLAR POTENTIAL — I. SPETGANG AND M. WELLS;
EDMUND SCIENTIFIC CO., BARRINGTON, N.J. 08007, 1976

<u>TECHNICAL</u>

<u>SOLAR HEATING AND COOLING: ENGINEERING, PRACTICAL DESIGN,
AND ECONOMICS</u> — J.F. KREIDER AND F. KREITH; McGRAW-HILL BOOK
CO., NEW YORK, N.Y. 10036, 1975

<u>ARCHITECTURAL</u>

<u>SOLAR ENERGY AND BUILDING</u> — S.V. SZOKOLAY; JOHN WILEY AND
SONS, NEW YORK, N.Y. 10016, 1975

<u>SOLAR HEATED BUILDINGS: A BRIEF SURVEY</u> (13TH EDITION, JAN. 1977)
W.A. SHURCLIFF; 19 APPLETON ST., CAMBRIDGE, MA. 02138, 1977

<u>GENERAL ENERGY</u>

<u>ENERGY FOR SURVIVAL</u> — W. CLARK; DOUBLEDAY AND CO., INC.,
NEW YORK, N.Y. 11530, 1974

<u>LOW-COST ENERGY-EFFICIENT SHELTER FOR THE OWNER AND BUILDER</u>
E. ECCLI, (ED.); RODALE PRESS, INC., EMMAUS, PA. 18049, 1976

<u>DIRECTORIES</u>

<u>INFORMAL DIRECTORY OF THE ORGANIZATIONS AND PEOPLE INVOVED IN
THE SOLAR HEATING OF BUILDINGS</u> — W.A. SHURCLIFF; 19 APPLETON ST.
CAMBRIDGE, MA. 02138, 1976

SOLAR ENERGY AND RESEARCH DIRECTORY—ANN ARBOR SCIENCE PUBLISHERS, INC., ANN ARBOR, MI. 48106, 1977

SOLAR ENERGY SOURCE BOOK—C.W. MARTZ, (ED), SOLAR ENERGY INSTITUTE OF AMERICA, P.O. BOX 9352, WASHINGTON, D.C. 20005, 1977

PERIODICALS

THE MOTHER EARTH NEWS—THE MOTHER EARTH NEWS, INC., 105 STONEY MOUNTAIN RD., HENDERSONVILLE, NC. 28739, BI-MONTHLY

SOLAR ENERGY DIGEST—CWO-4 W.B. EDMONDSON, P.O. BOX 17776, SAN DIEGO, CA. 92117, MONTHLY

GOVERNMENT PUBLICATIONS

BUYING SOLAR—FEDERAL ENERGY ADMINISTRATION; STOCK NO. 041-018-00120-4, SUPERINTENDENT OF DOCUMENTS, GOVT. PRINT. OFFICE, WASHINGTON, D.C. 20402, JUNE 1976

HOME MORTGAGE LENDING AND SOLAR ENERGY—D. BARRET ET AL.; STOCK NO. 023-000-00387-2, SUPT. OF DOCUMENTS, GOVT. PRINT. OFFICE, WASHINGTON, D.C. 20402, 1977

SOLAR DWELLING DESIGN CONCEPTS—AIA RESEARCH CORP.; STOCK NO. 023-000-00334-1, SUPT. OF DOCUMENTS, GOVT. PRINT. OFFICE, WASHINGTON, D.C. 20402, 1976

INDEX